Other Works by This Author

We're Off to See the Wizard

You Bet Your Life After Death

The Moment of Death

The 5th Secret

The 4 Secrets of the Universe

All About the Soul's Journey

The Book of Manifesting

Mysteries, Prophecies, and the Hollow Earth

The Lightness of Being

Sojourn

Poet Gone Wild

Poems of Life, Love, and the Meaning of Meaning

<u>Infinite Healing</u>

*Poems and Messages for the
Loss of a Loved One*

*Poems and Messages for the
Loss of Your Animal Companion*

SPIRITS SPEAK

PAUL GORMAN

Copyright © 2026 Paul J. Gorman
All Rights Reserved

Year of the Book
135 Glen Avenue
Glen Rock, PA 17327

ISBN: 978-1-64649-533-7 (paperback)
ISBN: 978-1-64649-534-4 (ebook)

Cover and interior photos licensed from Alamy, or public domain.

No part of this publication may be reproduced, distributed, or transmitted in any form or by any means, including photocopying, recording, or other electronic or mechanical methods, without the prior written permission of the author, except in the case of brief quotations embodied in critical reviews and certain other noncommercial uses permitted by copyright law.

Contents

Foreword 1
Introduction 3
Clara Bow 8
Stan Laurel and Oliver Hardy 11
Diana, Princess of Wales 16
Robert F. Kennedy 19
Frida Kahlo 22
Harry Houdini 25
Roberta Flack 28
Jim Croce 32
Peter Falk 35
Dean Martin 38
John Wayne 41
Dr. Jane Goodall 44
Judy Garland 48
Terry (Toto) 51
Margaret Hamilton 53
Ray Bolger 56
Jack Haley 60
Bert Lahr 63
Frank Morgan 66
Victor Fleming 68
King Vidor 73
Billie Burke 76
Charley Grapewin 80
Clara Blandick 83
Pat Walshe 86

L. Frank Baum	89
Elizabeth Montgomery	92
Hedy Lamarr	94
Rodney Dangerfield	97
Bob Marley	100
Humphrey Bogart	103
Lauren Bacall	106
Clark Gable	109
Carole Lombard	114
Albert Einstein	118
Lucille Ball	125
Sigmund Freud	128
William Conrad	132
Michelangelo	136
Frank Lloyd Wright	140
George Orwell	144
Linda McCartney	149
Cleopatra	153
Your Gift	157
Elizabeth Taylor	159
Steve Jobs	163
Message from God Mind	170
Peter Sellers	173
Florence Nightingale	176
Afterword	183
Affirmations	184
Biographies	186

Foreword

This is a book of my newest communications with the spirits of well-known and influential people who have died. It was written in the second half of 2025, after the publication of other spirit messages in *The Moment of Death – An Awakening into Awareness, Healing, and Love,* and also *You Bet Your Life After Death* – a comical, channeled 'quiz show' hosted by Mr. Groucho Marx.

Spirits Speak is a collection of 48 written conversations that I had with different spirits. A common theme they relate is that after death, they are no longer limited, and their minds are healed and aware – allowing them to hear the healed thoughts that we want them to hear.

Many spirits said that they were given options after death. One option was to choose a different outcome – and to re-enter their bodies a few moments before their death moment, and continue on living.

We always have choices – before birth, in every moment of our lives, and also after death. Death must be agreed to.

Our choices are always in our minds. Choosing kind, loving, and generous thoughts are an expression of what God is. In those moments, our minds are one with God, with no separation.

Being one with God, with no separation, allows us to manifest our desires.

The messages in this book are full of insights on consciousness, and how to live more effectively, as the aspects of God that we are.

Who would know better than those who have lived, made great achievements, died, and healed into vastly expanded awareness and love?

Introduction

I enjoyed writing the spirit messages in these chapters, and I find the discussions fascinating. Sometimes, I couldn't help wondering if I am dead also, because it seems that most of my conversations are with people who have died – the meaningful conversations anyway. My high school alumni page even had me listed as deceased. Hmm...

Oh well, deceased or not, I submit to you these accounts from the spirit world. Many of the messages talk about God and angels.

They say that we are each an aspect of God, having a dream of a life – but we don't believe that we're God, or that life is a dream.

Our dreams of life in the universe have infinite degrees of separation that are an illusion. When we die, so does the illusion, and all that we are becomes aware of itself as one again – in the Mind of God – not that it was ever not one.

As I received information, I would post excerpts on Facebook groups to share them. I was banned, blocked, declined, or booted off of every one – groups about 'Life After Death', and 'Promoting Spiritual Books', etc.

Maybe that's just my perception because I'm dead...which would explain a lot.

One fellow on Facebook was pretty angry, judging by his use of all caps, and profanity – "THERE'S NO SUCH THING AS GOD OR ANGELS!"

His rant was a full paragraph of rage and name-calling – and still in all caps, he declared that he had facilitated hypnosis over 121 times, and that no one ever mentioned 'God' or 'angels'.

Another person replied to him, "Why don't you post your findings then?"

Valuing my time and peace of mind, I left in one click, rather than argue with an unhealed mind – not that my mind is healed – but one of my Lifetime Agreements was to write books on how our reality manifests itself.

I didn't necessarily agree to promote the books, so I trust that people who need to read my healing information will manifest it.

When I asked my guidance about that incident, I received the message below. It seems that the hypnosis patients were not aware of God or angels because they were not dead, even if they had been regressed to a point in time before their births.

Is it possible that a person under hypnosis is not necessarily aware of angels or God because they do not have a healed mind?

A person who dies has a healed mind, which is opened in awareness and love, with no ego attachments. They usually report meeting angels, and being one with God.

All hypnosis therapy can heal is what is allowed to be healed by a person. Dying means all is allowed to be healed.

Why do hypnosis patients not report having contacts with angels?

Allowing a person access to their unconscious mind and asking questions, is like asking a car engine where it has to be going, and how fast – though it has no concept of distance or speed. It does not have that kind of information.

Hypnosis could be like looking at the world under the ocean, and channeling as looking at the universe that is in, which is mostly above the ocean.

Accessing a conscious mind has an unconscious half allowing itself and interconnecting communication that has not healed in a lot of ways. In a hypnotic communication, it can allow a lot of healing information to be revealed, but not more than is necessary.

Are angels real?

How would you define what is real?

Correct, because I'm living in a dream of time and space.

Dreams seem real, or they could not heal into an awakened state.

One of my spirit guides said that I had "found a pathway to God Mind," and am able access higher consciousness – as I think everyone does all the time.

I do not have details about levels of consciousness, or the subconscious mind. It seems to me that the subconscious mind is like the software that we have programmed, and our higher mind is God Mind and total awareness – not something that we have programmed – and our minds will become one with it in love and awareness, after death.

My belief is not to have beliefs – except for a belief in God, or love. It is what we are – in a world of love and non-love, lightness and darkness. Lightness and darkness are necessary for us to shine, and it gives us plenty of opportunities to heal. We chose our conditions as the perfect place to heal our minds.

The following chapters are arranged largely in the order that they were received. Often, I would start thinking about the deceased personality for a few days, and as I communicated with them, some revealed that they had prompted me to contact them. One acknowledged that he had one of my dogs wake me up in the middle of the night, at which time I wrote his chapter.

This book continues my exploration of spiritual concepts – about death, life after death, life as an individual dream, time as an illusion, and the holographic nature of our universe in a collective dream. You are not just appearing in it – you are at the center of it, and you are projecting the particular circumstances required to heal yourself in. It is as temporary as it is illusory, and illogical. It is illogical because we come from love, and it gives us the option to not love.

How can we each be projecting the universe, and also be in it? It is a magical mirror, and our healing projections of love create light – illuminating a new hologram for each of us in every moment. The light is infinite, and perpetuates the hologram. Shadows are not infinite. They are an absence of light, and they disappear as we project kind, loving, and generous thoughts.

Having kind, loving, and generous thoughts will magically create a new kind, loving, and generous universe for each of us in those moments.

It has to, because love is what powers the hologram. That is my understanding, from a perspective where I am not dead…well, at least not that I'm aware of.

Let's see what insights the healed minds of amazing spirits featured in this book have to say.

"Every journey is only inward," is what I say. All healing is only inward, on each of our healing journeys to oneness.

Clara Bow

Can I speak with Clara Bow, who died of a heart attack in 1965, at age 60?
I am Clara Bow. How may I help you? I can hear I am being asked if I can describe the ending of my life. I could have allowed myself a longer life, but I chose not to in my last moment.

I had been incredibly exploited throughout my life, and did not continue it for many other reasons. I had a lot of memories that made me ill when I remembered them.

How could I ever forget having them? I could have myself become another character in my acting, or I could die. It was that simple in my mind.

Were you greeted by an angel when you died?
A lot of angels came to meet me after my heart attack. All of them held me in their wings, one at a time, to make it the most healing homecoming I could have hoped for.

I loved each of the angel's comforting and healing words about how I could have anything, including a healed memory of my past. I said it is all I ever really wanted in my life. They explained how it made all of my achievements, and debilitated me at the same time.

I could not have been more healed than when I forgave myself, and everyone else in my life.

What happened after that?
An angel that had been my guardian throughout my life, and I headed away from the Earth, and I did not miss anything about my experience.

That is interesting, since you were the biggest movie star of the 1920s.
I could have been a big star, but I only needed a healed mind for my life to be a big success, and I did not achieve it.

What else would you like to say?
All I can be now is all I could have become in life – an aspect of God that has only one aspect – love.

*"We had individuality.
We did as we pleased.
We stayed up late.
We dressed the way we wanted.
I used to whiz down Sunset Boulevard
in my open Kissel,
with several red Chows to match my hair.
Today, they're sensible
and end up with better health.
But we had more fun."*

–Clara Bow

Stan Laurel and Oliver Hardy

Can I speak with Stan Laurel and Oliver Hardy about their deaths?
Oliver died of a heart attack in 1957, at age 65, after having had several strokes.
Stan died at home at age 74 in 1965, four days after having a heart attack.

Stan: How do you like that? I'm going to be in a book, Ollie.

Ollie: I am too. Let's see how we can make it memorable. Hello Mr. Gorman, how can we help you in your newest book writing?

Stan: I can hear him, Ollie. He said he wants to know how dying healed us.

Ollie: Oh, how nice. How did it heal us? I don't know, Stanley. You tell him how it healed us.

Stan: I healed because I didn't have a care in the world, making me healed and uncaring. I mean, healed and careless. I mean, careful not to be too careless and uncaring. That's how dying healed me, because I didn't care.

Ollie: How could dying make you not care? I cared about my life, and I cared about not dying.

Stan: I don't care. How do you like that?

Ollie: Oh, give me that hat (hitting him over the head with it). Now see if you care.

Stan: I care even less now, Ollie – now that you've messed up my hair. I am in heaven, and have no more cares, like I told you.

Ollie: After all I gave you, and that's the thanks I get – telling me you don't care because we're dead?

Stan: That's right – I don't care because we're dead.

Thank you, Stan and Ollie. Now, almost 100 years later, I think your films are seen more than ever because people have access to them all the time–on their phones that they carry with them.

Ollie: Their phones that they carry with them? How could they go very far, having a big box connected with a wire?

The newest communication technology has no wires, and the phones are small. They even have screens that you can watch any films on.

Ollie: Well, how do you like that? – a phone having film in it.

Stan: I know about that, Ollie. It doesn't have any film.

Ollie: It doesn't have any film?

Stan: It has a light in it, like we did when we were on the Earth. It can be internally projected, or it can be turned off–but it has a primary source of light, and local source for the power. Like I said, it's like when you and I had an idea, and it became our focus for entertaining people. It seems magical because it is magical. It is like God having a magical, healing instrument on the Earth – which was you.

Ollie: Now that's a fine mess I got myself into, Stanley. I had a magical, healing instrument – and it died.

Stan: I had mine, and it died also. It has to die, otherwise it would not be entirely magical and healing.

Ollie: How do you know so much, Stanley?

Stan: I don't know. I said I didn't care when I had a heart attack, and I was met by an angel who told me a lot of things I didn't know. I had to let it know if I wanted to go with it or not. I asked it where I would be going, and it said I could meet God if I wanted to.

Ollie: I had the same thing happen to me! I didn't meet God, have you?

Stan: I did, and God had on my hat. I asked for it back, and I got the strangest answer. God said I could have it, but I don't need it because I already have it. I said I didn't have it, but God said that I did. I scratched the top of my head, and God did it exactly as I was doing it – like I had a mirror in front of me, but it was all around me. I had my hat on, and so did God when I looked all around. I then had God tell me we are one and the same.

Ollie: Oh boy, Stanley – I mean God. I'm sorry I hit you over the head with your hat. How can it be that God and you are one and the same?

Stan: I am also one and the same with you, Ollie. I know it sounds magical, because it is. Now does it make sense how I don't have a care in the world? It had only been a projection in my mind, and in your mind, and in everyone's mind. They all have projections to heal in by overlapping them with other peoples' projections.

Ollie: How can I heal my projection, Stanley?

Stan: That is very easy, Ollie. Imagine that it is only your projection, and it doesn't need anything. If it doesn't need anything, then it only projects healing that is desired, but not needed. Healing means manifesting, because it doesn't need to heal. I manifest all that I imagine. It appears in my mind like the films we made.

Ollie: How come I am not one with God now?

Stan: I am one, and you are me. How can I ever be one without you?

Ollie: That's another fine manifestation you got us into, Stanley.

*"I had a dream that I was awake,
and I woke up to find myself asleep."*

–Stan Laurel

"If you must make a noise, make it quietly."

–Oliver Hardy

Diana, Princess of Wales

May I speak with Princess Diana, who died at age 36 in a car crash in Paris, in 1997?
All I can tell you has nothing to do with being a princess. "Nothing to do with being a princess" means I am an aspect of God, having no title or royalty.

I can help you in your consciousness research writing.

The world was shocked and saddened by your death.
I had been expecting for my life to be short-lived, even though I had the best care and protections. How did I know I was going to leave the planet prematurely? I had many dreams about leaving, and all of them healed me because I was not happy in my life. I had been in an arranged partnership, and then marriage and divorce. I had not had any love in my marriage.

You died in a terrible crash. Can you tell me your experience?
I had expected not to live long, as I had dreamed about. I healed in the dreams because I became a part of God again. In my death, I learned that I had exited a dream. In my dreams, I had been exiting life. I had it all backwards, meaning I could not have been happier to learn I had only been dreaming.

Please tell me what happened.
A motorcar crashing sound is all I heard in my advanced awareness, from above an accident scene. I heard a lot of people asking about Diana, and I had no

idea I was in the crash. I felt alive and exhilarated in my new awareness that I was not in a dream any longer. I comforted my children in their grieving moments. I had angels helping me, even though I felt as wonderful as I had ever felt.

Was your lifespan predetermined before you were born?
I could have extended it, but I had a period of time when it was most advantageous for me.

Did angels ask you if you were ready to go?
I had angels around me informing me that I could go back in time and continue my dream, but I had no interest in doing that then, or ever.

Thank you, Princess Diana.
I am Diana, Aspect of God, if you want a title. You are quite welcome Paul, Aspect of God – having a dream of not being God.

*"Anywhere I see suffering,
that is where I want to be,
doing what I can.
I want to be a queen
in people's hearts."*

–Princess Diana

Robert F. Kennedy

Can I speak with Robert F. Kennedy, who was shot and killed at age 42, in June 1968, at a political campaign event.
I am Bobby Kennedy. How may I help you?

I would like to ask you about your life ending when it did. Why did you die at that time?
I could have lived longer, and I also could have lived a lot less time than I did – it had to be completed in a certain period of time though.

Were you near the end of your agreed upon time?
I could have lived about 5 more months, but not any longer than that.

When was your approximate lifespan determined?
I had decided I could live between 39 and 43 years when I had chosen my lifetime, and made my Lifetime Agreements.

Can you tell me your main Lifetime Agreements?
"I could be honest with myself and my beliefs, even if my beliefs are contrary to most of my peers' beliefs."

Is there another one?
"All of my beliefs have an opposing belief that might also be true. Keep it in mind always when having a discussion with other people."

What did you feel after you were shot?
All I felt was lightness in my head, and nothing else because I was no longer living in my body.

"Lightness" means an all-encompassing healing love that has nothing else in it, with a beautiful feeling of having been totally supported in life.

Did you know you had been shot, and did you die immediately?
I did not realize I had been hit with gunshots until after I died, which had been a few seconds after being hit in the head with a bullet.

What would you like to say now, 57 years after your death?
I am no longer in a life having beliefs. Having beliefs makes them become your reality.

Thank you, Bobby.
I can hear in your mind if my son has support from me. He does, and he has chosen his belief in truthfulness.

*"There are those that look at things
the way they are, and ask why?
I dream of things that never were, and ask why not?"*

–Robert F. Kennedy

Frida Kahlo

May I speak with Frida Kahlo, who died in 1954, at age 47?
Acclimating in your mind now is Frida Kahlo, Mr. architect.

Correct. My career is being an architect.
A good one, I am being told by others in the spirit world.

It is mostly building codes and regulations these days, and they are hard to keep up with.
I am interested in the healing home you have designed.

I am getting the drawings of the particular geometry copyrighted, before publishing them. I'd like to build one also.
I can help in that regard. I had my home preserved after my departure from the Earth.

Thank you. Let's talk about your departure. Your last recorded words were, "I hope the exit is joyful – and I hope never to return."
That is a little bit of a mistranslation. I meant, I 'vowed' never to return.

Is that still true? Do you still vow never to return to the Earth?
I do. How's that for keeping my vows?

That is fine. You have free will, and the Earth is quite challenging – especially for an artist.

I am an aspect of God that has art to love in life, and art has nothing but beauty in it. How could I have been an artist, living in so much pain?

It is all I had for beauty in my life of mental and physical pain, where I had to let it out–not the pain, the beauty. More pain brought out more beauty, in my case.

Was your exit joyful?
I couldn't have loved it more. I was ecstatic in having left my body and lifetime concerns behind in a lifeless heap–making me see their true value, from my advanced awareness in my spiritual home.

What are you doing now?
Now I am having a conversation with an architect in the 21st century, and I can help him with the beautification of the Earth in architectural designs and constructions.

What other things do you do?
I can also have healing classes in my soul groups, where I am known for my beautiful expressions of life.

Can you tell me a little more about your death for this book?
I had an angel come into my head, at the moment I died. It had a lot of healing information for me, having lost my body in that moment of death.

How could I have been so wrong in my death conceptions in my paintings? I always had it be foreboding, and it is not that at all.

Do you mean the paintings with a skull and crossbones on your forehead? I love your painting, 'A Dance with Death', where you are dancing with a skeleton.
I love it also, because death is something I can dance with, having seen it for what it really is – an awakening into love and healing in God, having nothing else it can ever be.

Thank you, Frida.
I am thankful for this healing opportunity, meaning having readers see my new last words.

"Nothing is absolute. Everything changes, everything moves, everything revolves, everything flies and goes away."

–Frida Kahlo

Harry Houdini

May I speak with Harry Houdini, who died on Halloween in 1926, at the age of 52?
Death was likely from appendicitis, after being unexpectedly punched in the abdomen several times.
I am Harry Houdini. Have I had a moment trying to escape this conversation? I had, although I did not have enough courage to do so.

What do you mean?
All I could do in life was have an escape strategy, and after I escaped life, I could not escape all that I had always been – an actor in a dream, having only one escape. Does it make any sense?

In a dream it does. I dreamed I could escape from all limitations, but I escaped the dream, and do not have limitations anymore.

Was that your time to die? I guess it was better than dying in your escape act.
I could have died hundreds of times, but I chose to die in an instance of infection that had a lot of pain with it. How could I not have died when I did? I could have had a nice and easy home life in my retirement, and I would not want to escape from it – but I also could have been bored in my need for challenging achievements.

Was your lifespan predetermined?

I could have lived a little bit longer, but decided I could leave in the moment of debilitation, and having been hit in the belly unfairly. I did not have my guard up at that moment.

What was your dying experience like?
It had a lot of likeness to my acts. I entered into a lightness that had opened up in my head. It gave me all the freedom I could ever imagine. I had been living in a dream of limitations that I always tried to overcome.

Your last words were, "I'm tired of fighting – guess this is going to get me."
I had allowed my words to heal me in not having to fight in life, or in my life having no more need for fighting. How could I fight with life? It is not a wise activity.

Were you met by an angel when you died?
I was met by a lot of angels, having heard I was coming out of my body at that moment.

What did they say?
"Hello Harry, how did you get here?"

I said, "I didn't get here, I must have always been here."

The angels laughed at my answer, and said, "That is correct."

Great job, Harry. Do you have anything else you would like to say?

I can hear in your mind if I have any words of wisdom to add to your exploration of consciousness, life after death, and life in the spirit world. I can add new last words for my life...

"Life cannot be escaped – it can only be allowed. How can it be allowed, and not escaped? Because it has no escape mechanism, except for the realization in your mind that it is an illusion."

Thank you, Harry.
I am glad I could have this conversation with you. It heals me in my energy heart and soul.

"No prison can hold me;
no hand or leg irons or steel locks can shackle me.
No ropes or chains can keep me from my freedom."

–Harry Houdini

Roberta Flack

Roberta Flack was born in Black Mountain, North Carolina in 1937, and died in New York of cardiac arrest in February 2025, at the age of 88. Hello, Roberta.
A big hello to Mr. Gorman from Roberta Cleopatra Flack!

I was going to mention that – your middle name is Cleopatra, and Cleopatra is actually with me, in my mind. Maybe I should connect both of you.
I have been hearing her, and how you have been having her as your guest.

Cleopatra: I can feel how Paul loves Roberta's music, and her generous and gentle nature.

I do, and I grew up with her soulful songs. They are described as, "emotive, genre-blending ballads that spanned R & B, jazz, folk, and pop..."
Cleopatra: I heard a few of them in his mind. I love them.

Roberta: I healed when I sang them, and love it when I hear my songs in Mr. Gorman's mind.

You can hear them in my mind?
I can, and I do hear them because I am an aspect of God now.

I did not know that you were close friends, and next door neighbors with John Lennon, in the Dakota Building in New York.
I always admired him, and had even more admiration because I loved him, and Yoko and their son Sean.

Did you ever talk about recording a song together? You had made an album covering Beatles' songs.
I did not want to have it be my idea, but I had imagined how we would sound together.

This book is about returning to the spirit world – not that you ever left, so it is about leaving the physical world. Can you tell me what it was like?
I am allowing myself an instance of having a communication with a physical and spiritual being, making me heard in a physical being.

I am heard, and loved, and appreciated – healing me as a spiritual being, from a physical being. It is all I can get from a physical being, and all a physical being can possibly give to life, or anything in its life.

That's how it works – love life, and life loves you – because it is coming into creation as you.

That is profound wisdom.
I am an aspect of God now, and you are as well – but having a handicap in physicalness, allowing it to be an achievement in having the courage in life to allow all of life's challenges an appreciation for what they

are – your chosen healing, and loving, and allowing schoolwork.

I know I am in a hard school, the Earth school.
Making all 'A's' in your healing classes, at this level of higher education.

Thank you, Roberta. What was it like when you passed away?
I became illuminated in my head, because my body was no longer illuminating – I had died in a physical sense, but it made me more alive in a spiritual sense.

How could I have been more alive in my physical life? I could have allowed more of it, and appreciated it for what it had to heal in me. I could have loved it for gifting healing to me.

That is another profound insight.
I have another one, if you allow it in this communication.

Absolutely!
I had a lot of challenges in my life, being born when and where I was. All I had was my ability to sing, and I learned how to play a piano in my early years. I saw hate in the world, and did not have a reference to understand it in my mind. All I could do was focus on music because it was creative, and had beauty in its compositions and sounds. Allowing myself a creative outlet was my healing purpose.

Everyone has a creative, healing purpose, but many do not know what it is. All they need to do is ask their *higher self before their conscious mind goes to sleep, and the higher mind answers it – not only answers it, arranges the universe to creatively set it up for you.*

Wow–more profound insights.
If it is a practice taught to children, their life paths can be as they choose them to be.

Thank you, Roberta.
I thank you for giving me this creative, healing opportunity.

"Remember: Always walk in the light, and if you feel like you're not walking in it, go find it. Love the light."

–Roberta Flack

JIM CROCE

May I speak with Jim Croce, who died at age 30 in a plane crash? It was in 1973, in Louisiana – going from one concert location to another.
All I can hear in your mind is if I had agreed to my lifetime ending. I did – it cannot end without your agreeing for it to end.

Why did you agree for it to end – right at your peak?
I had another agreement that had nothing to do with my musical success. I could have delayed my death for many months, but I decided I would not likely have a better opportunity in those few months.

Was your lifespan determined before you were born?
I decided it in my last months, and I agreed I would not continue in my life on that last day, having played my last concert.

Why did you decide for it to end at age 30?
I had accomplished all I had set out to do in life, making it completed.

Was it just one agreement for your lifetime to be about 30 years long?
I had an agreement about its length, and about it abruptly ending. My lifetime had another agreement, and it was for my music to heal in the minds of many, many people. I kept my agreements, and left my life in

an instance of having nothing but lightness in my mind.

What about the 5 others in the crash? Did they have similar agreements about shortened lives ending abruptly?
They did – it cannot be anything other than what is agreed upon, although it can be modified.

Were you aware of the crash?
I did not have any idea, because I was looking down at it from my advanced awareness. I could discern an aircraft having been destroyed, and had no idea I could have been inside of it. My angel guide informed me, and I was relieved when I knew my agreements had been all fulfilled.

Thank you, Jim. Would you like to add anything else?
All I can add is how lucky I had been in my life to bring healing to the Earth, in my music.

"There's something about approaching universal truths with the simplicity of the acoustic guitar. You can take it anywhere, and it helps me reach listeners of all ages and all walks of life."

–Jim Croce

Peter Falk

Peter Falk died at home in 2011, at age 83, of pneumonia and Alzheimer's disease.
May I speak with Peter?
I am allowing my higher, healed aspect to communicate in your mind, if I may.

Yes, please.
All I can hear in your mind is if I am an aspect of God – or is God one mind, allowing us both to hear each other? It is the latter, and I am hearing a lot, if I focus on it.

What do you focus on?
I always have healing homework to do in my advanced state, having nothing else I could do.

Do you look for instances in all of your lifetimes to see how you could have been more kind and loving?
I do, all 854 of them. How could I have not been loving if I am God? I couldn't have been, could I? It was only a dream. How could I allow myself a dream having any non-love in it? I created it for my own benefit, to have myself discern God in it, or not. Discerning God in it heals the dream, making it not be illusory – but as real as it can get, being in a human body.

Can you tell me the purpose of this?
I can. In healing your dream, it heals the collective dream. Healing the collective dream will make it disappear. If it heals and disappears, God has nothing

to heal – which is fine, because it never did. It was only a game, having an infinite number of variables, except for one that cannot change – love, expressed in each mind, only in the present moment. It can be a feeling, or kindness in action. Nothing heals the dream more than kindness in action. It allows God an entrance into the dream–where it had not been until you allowed it in.

It's a challenging game, but is not challenging at all if we have kind and loving thoughts, because they make us one with God in those moments.

If you include kind and loving "healed" thoughts about all in your dream – including yourself – I would completely agree with your statement.

Thank you, Peter. Would you like to add anything else?

In a dream having love and non-love in it, become God-like by loving it for what it is – a dream of healing instances that are always in your mind.

Healing instances in your mind are God. It is that simple.

Thank you, Peter.
I am healing in the Mind of God.

"I could not chop down a tree
if my life depended on it."

–Peter Falk

Dean Martin

Dean Martin died at home in 1995, at age 78, of emphysema and respiratory failure.
His epitaph reads, "Everybody loves somebody sometime." May I speak with Dean?
I am allowing myself an instance of healing in a Gorman communication.

Do you know about Gorman communications?
I do, having heard I was going to be communicating in one of them.

Who did you hear it from?
I heard it from you, another aspect of God I am in communication with.

How will it heal you?
All aspects of God have a need for life, and life has a need for reflecting itself in consciousness.

If it did not have a reflection, it could not have any kind of reference in life to know itself.

I thought that God doesn't need anything.
God has no needs – only you have a need for God, because it is impossible for your life illusion to exist in existence if God did not have you needing to know where you originated from. If you did not need to know where you originated from, the illusion would have no meaning.

Finding its meaning is your purpose.

Where did I originate from?
All life had its beginning in the Mind of God as an idea of how could God ever need anything?

In creating an illusion of reference points, all consciousness became aware of itself in a holographic universe – making an infinite number of copies of itself in each moment, from your projection of it.

Keep going.
In each and every moment, there is a newly minted universe created by you – for only you to heal yourself in. I can describe it in movie terms, but it has to be in many dimensions, and filming is ongoing as you continue directing, acting, and writing whatever you want the story to tell.

How do I heal in it?
In the movie, have it be about awareness. How can I be a better actor and director, if I am the writer?

Write parts that bring out your highest qualities, and then act naturally.

The directing then becomes effortless, and the movie becomes a lifetime epic adventure, even if it does not have many locations.

How can we best write the next scene, while filming?
Allow it an instance of having no limitations in your mind.

How could I do this direction if I had an unlimited budget, and the universe would support me?

I could imagine I am God, and I am healed because I have no needs.

In imagining it, you are creating it as a new universe having no healing needs.

In your universe having no healing needs, it automatically grants your healed wishes.

Wow.
All I can add is to affirm it how you were going to write it.

"I am God, and I have no needs. I am healed, and the universe grants my healed wishes."
Action!

Thank you, Dean – for your profound insights.
I am healing in our communication as your assistant director.

"The good Lord gave me talent, and I'll use it until it runs out." –Dean Martin

John Wayne

John Wayne died of stomach cancer, in 1979, at the age of 72. May I speak with John?
All I will have known about my death is that it had me fooled. I thought I was going into a remission, having my cancer removed in a surgery.

What caused your cancer?
All cancers are a body's decision to have it listened to, how it has no need to kill itself.

A cancer has its beginning in a malignant thought, or belief. I got a cancer in my stomach by blaming myself for my failed marriages. I believed in my ability and desire for each of them to grow, and not die. My cancer grew, and I died because I did not accept my own forgiveness for all I had contributed to their failures.

Can you give me an affirmation for people to use, if they have failed marriages?
Affirmations heal in your accepting them. I believe I can give you one, having been in a number of failed marriages.

"All I am is all I am ever going to be – an aspect of God having healing needs in my mind. Allow my mind to heal in its love for itself, having no forgiveness needs to heal. Allow my love, having no healing needs, a home in my mind."

"My mind is peaceful. Love has a home in my mind. I do not need anything, and have no need for forgiveness."
I like it better in your healing words, than in mine.

I'll use them both–the more, the better.
I cannot disagree with that.

Can you tell me about your lifetime ending? Were you met by an angel?
In a cancer care center, there are a lot of people having angels appear. I knew one of them, and it was my angel in my lifetime – although I had no awareness of it until then.

I met with the angel a number of times, and it explained a lot that healed in my mind. I felt like I was getting a lot better after our interactions.

One day, it asked me if I could imagine being God, and all I could hear in my mind was, "How could I imagine being God?" All of a sudden, I had an incredibly intense light in my head, and I knew I was God in that moment. "How could I ever have had no idea?" was my next thought, and the angel and I ascended higher away from the Earth – although I was not in my body any longer.

Thank you, John. You are always admired for the strong film characters you played.
I had a dream that I was a strong film character. Healing myself by allowing self-forgiveness could have been my greatest strength, if I had allowed it. It

would have healed my mind, which would have healed my body.

Thank you, John.
Allow healing in my affirmation. It has enormous healing activation in it.

"Life is getting up one more time than you've been knocked down."

–John Wayne

Dr. Jane Goodall

Dr. Jane Goodall died at home of natural causes this month, in October 2025, at the age of 91. May I speak with Jane?
I am allowing a Gorman communication in my healed Light Mind, now that I am all healed, and all allowing.

Hello Jane, what lesson can you share with us about life?
I can hear in your mind about life being a healing dream, so the lesson is to heal it as you have chosen in your life's work, and in your relationships.

Can you give us a recommendation for healing?
Healing can only be in a person's mind, becoming like an animal having no healing needs in their minds.

Animals live in the present moment, love life, and love themselves. That is having healed minds.
An animal has a healed mind, making it one in God Mind. Humans have allowed a lot of interference in their minds to keep them unhealed.

I can hear in your mind that it is now more intense than ever, and likely a lost cause to heal humanity at this point. It can be a lost cause for many in your lifetime, but all have been in an agreement to heal in life, or heal in losing their life – so, it doesn't matter if they heal in this lifetime while living.

Wouldn't it be a greater achievement for their souls to at least try to become aware, and heal their minds?
All healing is in a person's mind, so it is in a person's best interest to introspectively heal it. Heal it by allowing only loving thoughts, and it makes all in your life become a healed instant in the Mind of God, that manifests all you desire in your life.

My books are all about that.
My life had been all about that also, having learned from nature.

Did an angel greet you when you died?
I had a lot of angels, and also a lot of animal spirits greet me in my moment of death. I had an amazing, healing reception in my initial entry into my eternal home in the Mind of God.

I read that your favorite animals were dogs, even though your lifetime was dedicated to studying primates, and doing groundbreaking research on chimpanzees.
I always had a love for my dogs – having only love, loyalty, and courage in their nature. I could not be in the company of people who did not like dogs.

I saw the beautiful video of a large chimpanzee that gave you a big hug, after being taken back out into the wild.
I had heard him cry of happiness in that almost impossibly poignant moment. It had made all of my efforts mean much more, in that moment of healing and gratitude. He had a long-held hope for himself, to

have another being that cared for him. It is how animals live and thrive in a family, or a closely-knit tribe.

Thank you, Jane – and thank you from the animals, the planet, and the people you spent your life helping and healing.
I am grateful for having lived among all having love in their hearts for caring to help conserve wildlife.

"What you do makes a difference, and you have to decide what kind of difference you want to make."

–Dr. Jane Goodall

Judy Garland

Can I speak with Judy Garland?
I am delighted I can be heard by Gorman in his mind.

Hello, Judy. I am writing another book about the moment of death. Can you please tell me what your experience was like?
I am sorry that you died at the young age of 47, and I really enjoyed your singing – especially in *The Wizard of Oz* movie.
I died from having too many anti-depressants in one night. What I needed had nothing to do with taking pills.

I needed a lot of love, and it had to come from inside of me, having no other place it could come from.

Did you know you had died at first?
I knew, and it didn't matter in my logic. I lived in the limelight, and would have traded it for love any day.

Did angels meet you?
I had been met in my mind by angels, and also a guide advisor who had always been with me.

He – if he had a gender – helped me throughout my life.

"Am I really dead?" is what I said to them, and they all said it was my choice if I wanted it.

I imagine it was like when you were Dorothy in *The Wizard of Oz*. The Good Witch Glinda said all you have to do is click your heels together 3 times, and say, "There's no place like home."
I had not considered it like that, but it was a lot like that scene.

Please tell me about your experience.
A guide, and my angels – of which there were four – all came into my head like it was a meeting about how I could live or die in the next moment, if I chose that option. Needless to say, I had decided I did not want to live any longer.

I was in a delightful, blissful world of lightness and lovingness.

As soon as I made my decision known, I had the most intense light in my head that pulled me into it all the way, from my head.

Then what happened?
I had died at that moment, and it was exhilarating, to say the least. I was God in that moment – all lovingness, and all peacefulness. "In that moment" is in all moments, because all in God is one instant.

Thank you, Judy. Would you like to add anything else?
I illuminate in love now. Be love, and illuminate God in life.

Terry (Toto)

'Toto' was a female Cairn Terrier, originally named 'Terry'. She lived from 1933 to 1945, and appeared in 17 films, including *The Wizard of Oz*.

May I speak with Toto?

I am a little dog named, 'Toto', or 'Terry'. I lived an entirely different life than most dogs and animals. I had a job, and I did the best that I could.

I live in a Light Body, and a Light Mind now, and I can hear how I am loved in my movie parts.

All I can hear in your mind is if I loved my life in Hollywood. I did love my life, and I cannot have anything but love for my life – in my earthly life, and in my spirit life.

I am a guide in having my lifetime movie parts heal in peoples' minds, allowing them to laugh at my antics. All of their laughter heals me in my spiritual home.

Thank you, Toto.
Call me if I can be of any guidance from my home in the Mind of God.

Margaret Hamilton

Margaret Hamilton died in 1985, at the age of 82, six months after entering a nursing home in Connecticut.
May I speak with Margaret?
I can hear if I am going to be an Almira Gulch character in this communication.

I had not had it in mind, but I could be another character having only love in my energy heart and mind. I couldn't be anything else, anyhow.

You are best known for your Almira Gulch/ Wicked Witch of the West character in the 1939 movie, *The Wizard of Oz*.
I am, but I had a lot more to offer as an educator of young minds.

I am writing another book about life after death. What can you tell me about that?
It has a lot of similarities to 'The Wizard of Oz', as I heard in your mind. I had not considered it like that, but now I know that it does.

All Dorothy had to do was decide she was going home, and a Good Witch allowed her entry into a land of her soul family. Death is almost the same thing, having an angel instead of a Good Witch.

All I can do is have healing thoughts, which is like Dorothy exclaiming how beautiful it was in her dream. In her advanced awareness, she had moments of introspection with her mind, her heart, and her courage. It is amazing in its analogous meaning.

Not healing moves her into another dream with her mind, her heart, and her courage.

In it, she can become confused by attacks from her ego demands, or flying monkeys in this film analogy. Her insistence on being lost is what keeps her lost, for her entire dream.

Almira, as the Witch, is the one who tipped her off to having her own personal power.

Her angel, or Good Witch, advised her not to give it away.

It is an excellent analogy for living in a dream.

Thank you, Margaret.
I no longer have an hourglass, because I am in timelessness – but in a dream, it can be as long as it has a purpose for healing your mind.

How would you recommend for us to heal our minds?
Imagine all of your life has been a dream, and dreaming has its advantages because it can be anything you imagine it could be.

"All I have is my power, and my angelic guidance. I direct my mind, my heart, and my courage to hear them only."

Affirming it makes it heal in your mind, which is having a dream.

Thank you, Margaret.
I am grateful for having this communication.

Ray Bolger

Ray Bolger died of bladder cancer in a nursing home, in 1987, at the age of 83.
May I speak with Ray?
I am allowing my heart and mind to have the courage in hearing Mr. Gorman's communication – having a degree in 'Thinkology', you know.

You were the best 'Scarecrow', Ray! It seems everyone was perfectly cast in the 1939 *The Wizard of Oz* movie, but you were originally cast as the 'Tin Woodsman'.
I am a dancer, not a mechanical man. I mean, I could not have been more poorly cast for being a Tin Woodsman.

You were an incredible dancer. There are videos online of you dancing in the 1930's.
Actually, I had a lot of hard times in doing some of those dance moves.

They looked impossible – especially the 180 – degree splits, where you then hiked yourself straight up a few times. The performances took incredible strength and agility.
All could have been a lot harder if I wasn't working on them all the time.

What would you like to say about *The Wizard of Oz* story?

It always had a lot of meaning for me, because I loved everyone I worked with in making the film, although I could not hear in my costume headgear very well.

If you represented Dorothy's mind, what did the Wicked Witch represent?
It had to be her fears of death, and losing her dog and family members.

That's a great answer. What do you think the Wizard represented?
The all-powerful Wizard had to be her imagining there could be another being having power over her life – even the fraudster character who could not help her in her despair.

Ray, can you tell me what happened at the time of your death?
I had a lot of pain in my bladder, not knowing it was cancer. Bladder pain is merciless in its debilitation. I had gotten a lot of medications, but nothing helped me to heal.

How come I got bladder cancer – I hear in your mind? I created it in controlling myself, by having incontinence – meaning no more control.

Incontinent means inconvenient.

Were you met by angels before you died?
I had been met in my dreams, and in my mind. Having no hope for healing my cancer, all of my angelic visitors counseled me on leaving my body behind. They all made it sound more appealing to leave my body.

One day, an angel asked me if I was going home, and I asked it, "How can I go home if I am cancer-ridden?" A light explosion hit me in the head, and I got the angel's message. I had gone home instantly.

How could I have been healed, and gone home – without leaving my body – I hear in your mind? I could have, if I had enough insight to heal my mind of its need for controlling my body. I needed the discipline for my dancing routines, when I had been dancing in my earlier years.

What happened after that?
Angels, and a few people I had known, came into my mind, and gave me a big welcome home party – like I had been gone for a long time.

Here is a little-known fact – I had never left. I forgot that I left, and like in 'The Wizard of Oz' movie, I had to find my way back.

I can hear in your mind, asking if I am in communication with Judy, and other members of the movie troupe. I am, and all have one healing message for everyone who is reading this – "Love is only in all that you have love for – it is the only place it can be."

That's perfect – thank you, Ray.
It is perfect – have it heal in your mind by loving all in your life, all of the time.

The time isn't real – only the love.

Jack Haley

Jack Haley died of a heart attack in 1979, at the age of 81.
May I speak with Jack?
All I can hear is if I had my heart attack because my heart had been broken.

I did, making me have one that is not breakable now.

Was life heartbreaking?
It is all about heartbreak, in my opinion. All heartbreak has one thing in common – it hurts having love in your heart, that cannot be loved in return.

Nothing in life is guaranteed, except that God will heal your heart. I had mine healed – it is as good as new – even better because it has no love limits, and it cannot be broken.

Can you please tell me what happened when you died?
I had a lot of heat in my head, and pain in my chest. All I could think was, "I'm not having a heart attack, I'm not having a heart attack." I did have a heart attack. I died immediately, and my body died shortly after that.

In my 'all awareness, healed in the light' stage, I could not have felt better. I still do, although I am one moment in God always, meaning eternally. I can allow this communication, and anything else I can heal my soul in.

Did an angel meet you when you had a heart attack?

An angel did meet me in my mind, giving me options. One option it gave me had nothing in it I was interested in. It said I could live, if I needed more earthly time, but I felt so good, I didn't need anything on the Earth.

The next option it gave me asked me if I could imagine God and myself being one.

I answered with, "No, I can't."

Incredibly, I became God – and have not been able to see myself as not-God again.

I am you, and you are God also. You just don't have my God-awareness testimonial.

You received "a testimonial" from the Wizard, in *The Wizard of Oz* movie.

All we had been given is what we already had. We did not know it had been there all along. That is how art imitates life. The movie characters looked for one thing they didn't believe they had in themselves – and looked outside of themselves for it to be given to them. In the end, it became clear they all possessed the qualities they had been looking for.

How could life be any other way? That is what life is for.

That's beautiful. Thank you, Jack.

I am all aware, and now healed from this Gorman communication.

Do aspects of God need to heal?
Not heal, but become one with God in one moment for me – and in all moments for you.

Bert Lahr

Bert Lahr died in 1967, at the age of 72. He was hospitalized for back pain, and it was reported that he died of pneumonia. His son said he succumbed to cancer, and the official cause of death was "massive intestinal hemorrhage." May I speak with Bert?

Aw shucks, I am in a Gorman communication. I am Bert – hello, Mr. Gorman.

Hello, Bert. Before we talk about life and your after – life, what happened at the time of your death?

All cancers have one thing in common – they grow until they can't grow anymore.

How could I have had cancer growing in my gut, and not been aware of it, I hear you asking?

I did have a feeling I may have cancer, but I decided I could live a normal life if I did not get cancer treatments that would have ended my life before the cancer did.

That is still largely true today, almost 60 years later.

All I can add is that cancer is more widespread and aggressive than in my lifetime.

What happened when you died?

I had an incredibly bright light come into my hospital room, and I had a good feeling when it was there.

It communicated with me in my mind, about how I could have all I ever desired, if I asked for it.

Of course, I loved hearing that. All I had to do was ask for anything, and allow it – and God would give it to me.

I needed my courage again, because I did not imagine that dying could be so beautiful, for me anyway.

It gave me all courage, love, and peace – wrapped in all awareness.

God gave it to me, meaning I gave it to myself.

Since you died, the importance and popularity of *The Wizard of Oz* movie has grown exponentially, and it is considered one of the best movies ever made.

It has humanity meeting inhumanity in the mean Witch character.

All of the characters had been invited into Dorothy's dream, and all had been included in it for her to heal them.

Thank you very much, Bert.
Courage has been given to all of life, making it your God-given nature.

Allow it entry into each of your thoughts and words.

Frank Morgan

Frank Morgan died of a heart attack in 1949, at the age of 59. He was found dead in bed. May I speak with Frank?

I am Frank – how may I be of assistance to you?

I already know how I can be of assistance, don't I?

Allow me to detail my adventures of chasing away death, and defeating almost impossible odds of ever making it to heaven – but I made it, and despite my treacherous journey, I am here to tell the tale.

Thank you, Professor Marvel!

I am not a marvel, you can be sure of that – but I have one thing that is marvelous.

I am God, having a dream that I am you – and you have figured out that I am you having a dream.

Can you tell me what happened when you died?

I died in my bed. If I had to choose a place, that was it. How could I choose a place?

"Leave that to me," is what I always said. Life is all about having a choice – and choices are healing, or hurting in each moment.

How could I choose my location at the time of my death?

I chose it before I was born, having decided I was going to die in my bed, in my sleep.

Is there a better choice?

You are right, that is the best choice. Did an angel meet you?

A lot of angels, and a number of friends had met me on my entry into the spirit world.

I did not have a long list of deceased friends, but there were a few I had close friendships with, that had died before me.

In retrospect, I know that I, and they did not die – all we did is become lighter in our perspectives.

Lightness is the Mind of God.

I can hear in your mind – what was the role of the Wizard in Dorothy's dream?

In her dream of life, her mind kept searching for answers outside of herself.

All of life's answers are inside of each person – and it happens to be where God is, and answers them.

Thank you, Frank.
I am always inside, giving answers as God. Nothing can be gained unless you ask.

Victor Fleming

Victor Fleming died of a heart attack, on the way to the hospital in Arizona, at the age of 59. May I speak with Victor?
I am Victor Fleming. How may I be of assistance in your consciousness research?

I am writing a book of messages from spirits of people involved in the 1939 making of *The Wizard of Oz* movie. What would you say is the theme of the movie?
I made it because I love its contrasting love and evil in its characters, and in having them all in Dorothy's mind. Nothing had been more important in the world at that time.

Those are really great points. It remains as one of the best movies ever made.
I am glad about it being a popular movie for each generation after its release.

You had a wonderful cast and crew.
I had a lot of help, meaning it is not my creation – although I did have my say in directing each scene.

You died at the relatively young age of 59, right after filming *Joan of Arc*.
I died because I had no more movies to make, that I could be proud of.

You could have retired, or trained others in movie – making.
Good point, but I also could have been defeated having no more creativity in myself, at my older age.

I can hear you asking if I think that is a true statement. It is not true, and I can tell you the truth.

I could have been more creative than ever, because I had a lot of experience in my craft. I could have hired a lot of the most talented people in the business also.

Life has its lessons, and mine was not giving in to fear and doubts.

How can I answer you if I am being asked another question?

Sorry.
I am hearing you ask if my lifetime had an ending date that had been planned in advance, or even before I came into my life. It had a long, or a wide range of time that could have been about 19 years longer, if I wanted it to be.

Did an angel meet you when you died, or ask you if you wanted to continue on living?
It did. How did you know to ask me that?

It is very common, or even standard for people to be given choices at the moment of death.
All I could have chosen was not to be in my dying body anymore. I could have gone back to before having a heart attack, and lived in a normal fashion, but I chose not to.

Did you prefer the feeling of total love and awareness, with no earthly concerns?
I did, and always will, in my eternal home.

Was the angel that met you your guardian angel?
It had been a guardian angel in my lifetime, and I hear you asking its name. It is 'Landin'.

Thank you, Victor.
I can add one more piece of information for you to write.

I am an aspect of God, within an aspect of myself, which is within an aspect of you and everyone else.

Where is that aspect within me?
It is in God's aspect, which is you – meaning it can only be in your mind, which lives forever.

Can we only access our God aspect with kind, loving, and generous thoughts?
Always – how can it be anything other than kind, loving, and generous thoughts?

It cannot – except for in nature which cannot be unkind, or unloving.

I teach people that having kind and loving thoughts – which exist only in the present moment – make us one with God Mind. When we are one with God Mind, there is no separation, and we can manifest our desires.
All correct, although God Mind has no desires – only you can have them.

In life, it gives you choices of what to desire – God, or all that is anti-God.

"Anti-God" is all non-loving thoughts in your mind.

I can hear in your mind – that is how Dorothy learned her life had been a dream.

She confronted her fears – and healed her mind, her heart, and her courage.

Thank you, Victor – for creating that timeless movie, which is a perfect metaphor for life.
And life after death – meaning how could death be real, if life is only a dream?

KING VIDOR

King Vidor directed the last 3 weeks of primary filming, and the Kansas scenes for *The Wizard of Oz*. He died in 1982, at the age of 88.
The previous weekend, he and former lover Colleen Moore had driven up to San Simeon, William Randolph Hearst's 'Castle' to watch home movies made when they had been Hearst's guests there, 60 years before.
May I speak with King?
About my having been in 'The Castle' – I had had a loving and committed relationship with Colleen in my younger years, but did not have relations with her after that. I can make the record straight.

That's fine.
I can also have it known how my directing in 'The Wizard of Oz' had been like making a film about how Dorothy allowed her imaginations, fears, and her dreams to become her reality.

In imagining how her life could be, in her 'Over the Rainbow' singing, her dream had its formation.

In it, her dream has Bluebirds that became a lot of Flying Monkeys – and they destroyed her heart, her mind, and her courage. How could her mind, her heart, and her courage be defeated by monkeys?

Her monkey attackers had known about her location, and her defenselessness against them.

Each monkey had been one of her fears, and all came from her one innermost fear of being separate from God. All she could do was have her mind, her heart, and her courage protect her, but they were not equipped to deal in fighting against wickedness. It was her dog that had been clever enough to help her.

What did her dog, Toto represent in her dream?
It had been her constant companion – and loyal to her, no matter how many others had been around.

It could have been her connection to her higher mind, which is her God-self – meaning her spirit, or soul's aspect of God.

That's an excellent answer. Thank you, King.
How did her dog appear in her lifetime dream? It escaped from a basket, and made her a vulnerable target for the evil witch. All she had to do to avoid her ordeal was to keep her mind, her heart, and her courage alert – so her dog, or God-self did not get away.

Awesome – you gave me a significant insight into one of the movie's lifetime metaphors.
I had directed the scenes where her dog is in Kansas with her.

The Kansas scenes are fantastic.
"How can it be a dark contrast to her dream?" had been my direction.

Let's talk about your lifetime dream. What was it like when you died?

I had died and awakened from my dream also. I was not awakened by my dog, or God-self. I had been awakened 'into' my God-self, by my God-self calling me home, like Dorothy being home again.

How I can describe it is if a person can be blasted high into the air, and the air is all love, and all awareness. It is an exhilaration that cannot be imagined.

Did an angel meet you then?
I had a lot of angels, and a number of friends and relatives meet me in my God-self home of all love and awareness. It is like Dorothy's home in the final scene, where her family had been all along – none of them having ever left, including Dorothy.

Thank you very much, King – and for your contributions to *The Wizard of Oz*.
It has been delightful, Mr. Gorman.

BILLIE BURKE

Billie Burke played 'Glinda, the Good Witch of the North' in *The Wizard of Oz* movie. She died of Alzheimer's disease, at age 85 in Los Angeles, California, in 1970.
May I speak with Billie?
I am Billie Burke having a communication in my Light Mind, having no more life-mind, or body.

All I can hear is, am I alright having died from Alzheimer's? I died of old age. How could I have lived much longer?

It depends on what you call living – and if dying illuminates you in God, then how can it be called "death"?

Great points.
How can I be helpful in my illuminating God in my Light Mind? I am illuminating God in my Light Mind, which is illuminating in your Light Mind – which is illuminating in your life-mind, or left brain.

I hear your life-mind asking, how can I be better in illuminating information from my Light Mind, or right brain?

Begin by imagining a light in the middle of your brain. It is God, in a blue-magenta light that you know about.[1]

Allow it to increase in intensity in your mind. Alternate in having it illuminate each half of your brain, allowing each instance of illumination to heal the other half of the brain.

After alternating for about 10 minutes, the light illuminates both brain hemispheres.

All having both hemispheres illuminated will become God- like in their projections of their realities.

Wow – that is a great exercise, and complements what I know about God, the brain, and manifesting with light – all of which project our realities.

All in my communication here has been a lightness illuminating in part of your left brain, as it is allowed into your right brain.

Is there any way I can enhance that, other than with the alternating lightness exercise that you described?

Allow only lightness into all of your thoughts, and lightness is what heals all of your projections – allowing them to manifest in reality.

Thank you, Billie. Can you please tell me what happened when you died?

---

[1] Discussed in *The Book of Manifesting*, 2024

As I was communicating to you, I did not die – I became alive in a moment of awakening, having no earthly attachments, allowing me to fly.

I hear in your mind asking – did an angel meet me in my God-like awareness, now that I had no body to hold me back?

I had a lot of angels, and also my friends and husband who had predeceased me.

What happened next?
I hovered over my deceased body for a while, and decided I did not need it any longer.

Did it seem like "a while" to you?
It could have been about 5 minutes, but I cannot measure in a timeline now.

Did you return to your soul groups?
I did, and I am always in my groups, having lessons instilled into my soul.

I almost forgot to ask you about *The Wizard of Oz* movie. What did 'Glinda, the Good Witch of the North' represent in Dorothy's mind?
Glinda healed Dorothy's fears by giving her life-mind its own powerful connection to God back.

God in the movie was all of the other characters healing in her mind – and having the evil character, meaning the bad witch, melt away into nothing but pure water. God is Dorothy healing in the moment she cared more about being home, than being in a dream trying to find help to get her there.

Wow – that's awesome. I never knew where God was in the movie. I think Glinda was her higher self, and the little people were her thoughts – all convinced that she was lost.
I agree, and all of the little people had hope for Dorothy to get home.

Thank you, Billie. Would you like to add anything else?
In life, heal all that is fearful because it is an illusion that is only in your dream for you to heal it.

Charley Grapewin

Charley Grapewin played Dorothy's 'Uncle Henry' in *The Wizard of Oz* movie. He died of natural causes in 1956, at home in California, at the age of 86.
May I speak with Charley?
All I can hear is how did Uncle Henry fit into Dorothy's dream of a life?

I had been a guiding force in her life, because her parents didn't appear, did they?

That's a great point – I never noticed they were missing.
How could her parents have fit into her dream of a life? Her parental figures were myself
and Aunt Em – plus a few farmhands, having befriended her in the movie.
Thank you, Charley. You had an impressive acting career, having been in over 100 films. You were also a Vaudeville and circus performer, a writer, and a stage actor.
All I ever had an interest in was acting – not in films necessarily, but acting on a stage.

Can you tell me what it was like when you died?
In my life, I had never thought about death, although it had been all around me.

Dying had been a lot like Dorothy going home – but imagine it having only love, all awareness, no fear –

and death is not even a concept, other than awakening in God.

How could death even exist, if life had been a dream of having been separated from God?

That's a great point. Did angels meet you when you died?
I had one angel meet me in my awakening into all awareness. It had been my angel and guardian in life. It asked me if I knew my life was ending. I answered it in the affirmative, because how else could I have met an angel?

I could have, but did not know how I could have, in my lifetime dream.

How can we meet angels in our lifetime dreams?
All you have to do is ask your angel to heal all in your mind that needs healing, and it will heal it in God's love – although you have to ask for its help, and allow its healing. A healed mind is higher in consciousness, and can see angels.

Did you proceed away from the Earth with your angel?
I could have, but I was awakened from my dream of Earth living.

Thank you, Charley.
You are healing in your dream, as one who has an interest in awakening from a dream – while still being in it.

Clara Blandick

Clara Blandick played Dorothy's 'Aunt Em', in *The Wizard of Oz* movie. She died of suicide in 1962, at the age of 85.
May I speak with Clara?
I am Clara. Hello, Mr. Gorman. I expected I would be in your book of healing messages, since I had been Dorothy's 'Aunt Em' in The Wizard of Oz movie.

Hello, Clara. I was surprised to learn that you took your own life. It was reported that you dressed immaculately, then took an overdose of sleeping pills. You had left a note that read, "I am now about to make the great adventure. I cannot endure this agonizing pain any longer. It is all over my body. Neither can I face the impending blindness. I pray the Lord my soul to take. Amen."
Your ashes are interred just yards away from our last guest, Charley Grapewin.
I died in my sleep, and I awakened in heaven. I could have lived a little longer, but I had no desire to.

Was it like when Dorothy awakened from her dream of a life?
I had always wondered what it would be like when I died, and I didn't expect for my death to be as exhilarating as it had been, and still is. I felt like I had been in an airtight container, unable to breathe – and

then I exited it into an atmosphere of fresh air and sunshine, having no container at all.

It was way better than Dorothy's awakening in the closing movie scene.
I agree, but Dorothy's closing scene had her surrounded by love – that is accurate.

Thank you, Clara. What else would you like to add?
I had been an actress in my life, but now I am not acting at all. I am an all-aware aspect of God, that has no need to act. I only have healing desires, much like in life – but I am aware of it now.

I hear you asking – what caused my arthritis, and losing my eyesight?

I had a lot of heartache in my divorce, and in my life after my divorce. All I had in my life for companionship were my acting companions.

Would you like to add any advice for people?
Acting has its advantages, if you are acting in a dream, knowing it is only an act. The advantage of acting is knowing that it is only an image you are projecting.

In God Mind, there is no image – only an imaginary dream, having images to heal.

Thank you, Clara.
I am appreciative of your including me in your book of messages from our acting cast, and production crew.

Pat Walshe

Pat Walshe played 'Nikko', leader of the Winged Monkeys in *The Wizard of Oz* movie, because of his animal impersonating skills. He died of a heart attack in Los Angeles, in 1991, at age 91. He was the last surviving cast member of *The Wizard of Oz*. May I speak with Pat?

How can I help you in writing about how I had been a Flying Monkey in the movie?

I had a lot of good luck in my life, especially in that role. I gave it all I could in acting how a monkey acts.

All I can hear you asking is if I had a lot of work in preparing for that role. I could act like a monkey, but I had to 'be' a monkey for that role. To 'be' a monkey, I had to live like a monkey for a few months before filming began. I would go to hear and watch the monkeys in a zoo, as much as I could – and it gave me a lot of insight on how they would react to each other. I memorized all of the inflections in their movements, and in their having nothing but animal minds. I became like a monkey in my mind, when I was alone.

It was hard to believe that it wasn't a monkey in the movie.

I gave it all I had, as I said.

This is a book about our journeys out of this life. Can you tell me what it was like when you died?

I can describe it – and describing it is not going to be as incredible as it is – but I became a light being.

My body became insignificant, and unnecessary. It had been my animal costume – for imitating animals, if that makes any sense. All I could have hoped for in life had been accomplished, and my life had been completed in my dream of it.

What did the Winged Monkeys represent in Dorothy's mind?

All of her ego demands, and ego judgments of herself that debilitated her mind, her heart, and her courage.

Her heart, her mind, and her courage – along with her dog – helped her to defeat the entire kingdom of the Wicked Witch.

Is it because she was an aspect of God, and the Land of Oz in her dream was an illusion?

I can agree with it, now having a God insight into what you are writing.

Thank you, Pat. Would you like to add anything else?

In life, it is not necessary to have incidents of healing your mind, heart, and courage – they are all that you are. You only have to overcome the ego demands that hide them.

L. Frank Baum

Author L. Frank Baum had a stroke, slipped into a coma, and died the following day, at the age of 62. It was in 1919, nine days before his 63rd birthday – and 20 years before *The Wizard of Oz* movie was made. He wrote 'The Wonderful Wizard of Oz' in 1900, and a series of 13 more 'Oz' books, that were published up until 1920.

May I speak with Frank?
"All I can believe, is all I can become." That had been my belief in life.

I am hearing – how did I have a stroke, at only 62? I could have lived a little bit longer, but I had made an agreement before I was born, to leave before my 63rd birthday.

Why did you pick that particular age limit for your life?
All I could have done had nothing to do with my age. Age is an agreement, like everything else.

It is an artificial construction, having nothing in it that is meaningful, other than what you give it.

I decided I could complete my goals in that amount of life – meaning I could heal my mind in that amount of time.

I do not know if *The Wizard of Oz* movie is true to your book themes.
It has a lot of analogous interpretations, but I did not have it ending the way that it did.

Can you please tell me about your lifetime ending?
An angel came into my head, and it gave me another option for living in my debilitated condition, or to continue on as I had already agreed. I did not have an interest in continuing on in my debilitated condition, meaning I had accepted that I was going to die, and continue on with the angel.

What did you feel?
I felt an all-encompassing love, that I cannot begin to express in words.

I can hear in your mind, asking how I am doing, now that I'm dead. I'm doing all that I ever dreamed I could do, making my death the most loving, and healing experience I could ever have hoped for.

It is a little bit tricky because I manifest everything I think of, even if it is not for my healing – much like in life, but in life there is a lag time. Manifesting in life allows a person his or her own desires a birth in life, or not.

How can it be healing if it is any other way?

All I can hear in your mind is – how is life like the movie of my books? I am hearing in your mind that the movie was made long after I had died. I can access any information in my advanced awareness.

I loved a lot in the movie, except for the apple orchard scene. Apples are not evil like the Adam and Eve story.

In an evil apple orchard, they would not have wanted the apples from the tree.

Having the apples would have made them highly incapable of defeating the evil witch.

That's a really great point.
It cannot be deleted now.

Thank you for your input, Frank. Is there anything else you would like to say to the readers of this book, that is being written in 2025?
"All I can believe, is all I can become" – in a lifetime dream, or in an afterlife awakened.

Having it in both is all you can ever be. Believe in your ability as God, to be all that your heart desires.

Allow your heart, your mind, and your courage to guide you.

Elizabeth Montgomery

Elizabeth Montgomery died at home in Beverly Hills, of colon cancer in 1995, at the age of 62. She may have something to tell me.

All I am hearing is if I have something to tell you for your writing about having lost my life in my early 60s. I can tell you I do, and have a lot I can share here.

All I can hear in your mind is, am I okay having lost my cancer battle, in my lifetime of blessings and good fortune? Actually, I had my biggest blessing in the moment I died. I could not have asked for anything more than being home in the Mind of God, once again.

How could I ask for anything, if I don't need anything? It is not logical for God to have a need for anything — that is what humanity is for.

Humans have one, and only one choice in every moment. Is my choice healed in my mind, or does my choice need healing in my mind? Healed choices have love of life in them. Unhealed choices do not have love of life in them.

"Life" means all of life, including yourself.

Highly advanced beings are here now to instruct you further. Michael, the Archangel is here with you now.

"I am Michael, archangel in the angelic realm of highly illuminating beings. I can guide you in healing your mind, having nothing else I can do, unless called upon."

Thank you, Archangel Michael – please do.
"A healed mind has no needs, so I will not ask you what you need. I know how I can be of healing assistance to you though. I have love I can instill into your mind for life.

Having love for life – for life – makes your mind totally healed. How could it be any more healed?

A healed mind is one with God Mind, so it cannot be more healed. You also can manifest all of your desires. Allow all healed desires into your life, as each one appears in it.

Love it as it is now in your life."

Thank you for everything, Archangel Michael.
"I can also give another loving message to you from Elizabeth Montgomery. Her message is this – 'Loving life can also mean not needing it – or losing it. Having life means not having to hold onto it. It holds onto all it can ever hold onto, which is love for itself'."

Hedy Lamarr

Hedy Lamarr died in Florida in 2000, of heart disease, at the age of 85. May I speak with Hedy?
All I can hear in your mind is how beautiful I had been in my life. I had a lot of fun in my life, but I also had a lot of heartbreak. Although I had beauty, I made a lot of inventions – one of which helped the Allied Forces in the Second World War.

I know – congratulations, and thank you.
I can hear in your mind how my invention may have helped in a lot of unseen ways, even if it was not apparent in its working to defeat Germany. I can detail it now from my advanced awareness.

I am reading that your 'Secret Communication System', patented in 1942 for radio frequency hopping, was not used by the Navy in World War 2.
Actually, it had been extensively tested, making it definitely used in World War 2.

I am reading that you were considered the most beautiful woman in the world, and had a number of failed marriages and strained family relationships.
I did, and it gave me heart disease in my later years.

Can you tell me what it was like when you died?

I could not have felt more ecstatic than having left my body and earthly cares behind. God had given me a lot, and it was not a lot compared to my dying gift of healing and awareness, and incredible love that I could never find in my life.

Did an angel meet you?
An angel had been around me for my entire life, and I know how it helped me – in my despair especially. It asked me if I could imagine myself with God, and I couldn't. It asked me if I could imagine myself being one with God, and I couldn't imagine it either.

In that moment, my head had the most intense light in it, and it pulled me into it. I met God, and God had been in me – and was me all along. I did not have the awareness of God being me in my life, like I do in my advanced awareness.

What would you like to say to people now?
All healing can only be in your mind if you allow it. Allowing God is what you are allowing. God can be allowed or disallowed. It is up to each person in every moment – that's where God really is.

Thank you very much, Hedy.
Although I am Hedy, I am also God, having been allowed to communicate through you.

"I was madly in love with life."
—Hedy Lamarr

Rodney Dangerfield

Rodney Dangerfield died in 2004, at the age of 82, from surgical complications. On the day he died, a randomly selected Joke of the Day on his website happened to be, "I'll tell ya', I get no respect from anyone. I bought a cemetery plot. The guy said, 'There goes the neighborhood'. "His wife used that as the epitaph on his grave marker. May I speak with Rodney?

All I get is no respect from anyone, not even from my guardian angel. It asked me if I knew I was dead. I said, "How could I know I am dead, if I am dead?" I get no respect at all – it said I could know I was dead because the audience is still laughing at me.

How do you like that? – having a clown as my guardian angel. I tell ya. It doesn't get any easier being me, even if I am dead. I asked God if I could finally get some respect. Get this, God said it had a lot of laughs at my comedy – the only difference in my being dead is not being a stand-up comic.

I gotta tell ya, that's how I get treated around here – no respect at all.

That's hilarious!
I don't get any respect here. God heard my angel being a clown, and gave me a circus tent to have for an eternity. I said, "How come I got a circus tent?"

God said, I'm gonna need it for my lifetime healing review – everybody's coming to hear me laugh at myself.

I said, "I don't get it."

God said, that's why I'm here, so I can get it.

I said, "Get what?"

That I am God, and can only laugh at myself in Oneness – is what God said.

How do you like that? "If I am God, then why didn't I get it?" – is what I asked God.

Because if I get everything, then I would be everything – and being an individual couldn't be everything – was God's answer to me.

"How could I be everything?" – is all I could think of.

God said I could be everything if I got out of my clown costume, and gave it the respect it deserves, and then leave it behind as a lifetime memory.

Thank you, Rodney.
I am God now, and how's that for getting some respect?

*"I'm not afraid to die.
I just don't want to be there when it happens."*

–Rodney Dangerfield

Bob Marley

Bob Marley died of cancer in 1981, at the age of 36. His last words to his son Ziggy were, "On your way up, take me up. On your way down, don't let me down." May I speak with Bob?
I can hear – I am Bob Marley.

Hello Bob, do you know what I want to ask you about?
About my afterlife, but I am not dead – just gone from a cancerous body, having nothing I could need it for.

What caused you to get cancer, and die young?
I had a lot of heartache in my life. Although I had a lot of money, I could not help my countrymen, and women, and children in a way that could bring them all that they needed for their own wellbeing.

I was in Jamaica in the mid-1980s, and a lot of the people lived in poverty. I don't think it has changed a lot.
All have an agreement to heal themselves in a land having little, or no assistance.

Can you tell me what it was like when you died?
All I had in my head was, "How did I get here?", and "How could I have healed myself in my body?"

Not having an answer, an angel being gave me a lot of insight by asking me, "How did you become a light being without healing in your body?" I did not have an answer, but it gave me an insight.

I had always been a light being, having nothing to heal but my mind – which would heal my body. I had not healed my heart, or my mind in my last few years of life.

Was your lifespan predetermined?
I could have allowed for it to be extended, but I chose not to.

What did you feel when you died?
I felt like I had been in a dream, and was awakened with a bucket of warm water thrown on me – and it was magical healing water, and all it touched became loving awareness. Have it heal in your life by allowing it, and inviting it to heal you, and cleanse everything that is on your mind – and it will.

That's beautiful – thank you, Bob.
How else may I help you in your writing?

You can tell me.
I can heal all in your mind if you allow me to, and ask me to.

Yes, please do. Thank you, Bob. I'm going to play 'One Love' and more of your reggae songs today.
I am already hearing how they will heal in your mind.

Is there anything else you would like to add for readers of this book?
All God can be is all God can ever be – a healed, loving, kind, or generous thought – and only in your mind.

"You never know how strong you are, until being strong is your only choice."

–Bob Marley

Humphrey Bogart

Humphrey Bogart died of esophageal cancer in 1957, at the age of 57. May I speak with 'Bogie'?
How did I become "Bogie"? I'm not even in Hollywood anymore. Hello Gorman – how can I help you?

I am communicating with spirits of well – known and interesting people who have died. The information will be in a book about death, and life after death.
Allow Bogie an interesting entry into it. I always had an interesting story for my friends and acquaintances.

Let's hear your story.
I had been minding my own business, when I heard a loud banging on my forehead.

An angel had been trying to get my attention.

"Bogie, Bogie – it's me. I know you can hear me," is what it said.

Ha!
I opened my eyes, and it really scared the crap out of me. An angel was about an inch in front of me, and it was glowing. "I have a lot to discuss with you", it said.

I didn't know what I could do – I couldn't even get out of bed.

In an instant, I had an explosion of light in my head – and now I happened to be in an upright position, talking to the angel. "How did I get here?" I asked.

"Here is everywhere", the angel replied.

I could see my body in the hospital bed in that moment – not having more than one moment, if that makes any sense. Not having any more moments – there had to be only one explanation.

I had died, and was in an eternal moment in the Mind of God.

That's a great story. Thank you, Bogie.
I didn't finish – here is the interesting part.

In my eternal moment, God and I are one. I know how it sounds – like I am God, and I am omnipotent – but I can reassure you that you are too. All God has for healing is humans. Other than that, it is a giant illusion for them to heal in.

That is my understanding – we are individual dreamers in a collective dream, and only God is real – which is expressed as kind, loving, and generous thoughts. Those kind, loving, and generous thoughts heal our minds, and make us one with God in those moments. Then there is no separation.
All I can add is a little bit of God wisdom. Nothing has a purpose. Imagine having nothing in your dream.

It couldn't be a dream, could it? I gave it a giant backdrop to heal in.

Thank you for your interesting insights and story, Bogie. By the way, one of my favorite

movies is *Key Largo*. I had a framed movie poster in my office.
All I can hear is how cool it looked in your office. I enjoyed being in that movie, and having it be enjoyed by millions of people, over a lot of years in Earth time.

Now I can hear in your mind how Lauren Bacall will be your next guest. I can notify her.

Thank you, Bogie. Is there anything you would like to add for the readers of this book?
I am all, and I am all having a dream that I am you having a need for healing – by finding where 'all' really is.

How can I be all without you? I cannot. That is why it can only be in a dream.

"Ain't nothing a man can't do
if he believes in himself."

–Humphrey Bogart

Lauren Bacall

Lauren Bacall suffered a stroke, and died in 2014, at the age of 89. May I speak with Lauren?
I am Lauren, and Bogie alerted me to your communicating with me, after you had communicated with him.

Yes, he gave me great insights on consciousness, with his interesting story about his death.
He didn't believe he could die, and now I know he was right – we don't die. All we can do is awaken from a collective dream, by healing our individual dreams – in life, or in death for most people.

Would you call the Earth a hard school, and that you have to be an advanced soul to incarnate into it?
All advancement is in your mind, so it is not a school – you are. All souls are advancing, and at different levels – so many have not advanced much at all.

Great points. How is a person's mind a school?
It registers for certain classes in particular fields of study. It advances in developing its own curriculum – and healing and instilling all it has learned. Not healing in life heals in death, which could be like a graduation.

Can you please tell me what it was like when you died?

I had been having migraine headaches for about a week, when I became incapacitated by a stroke. I did not become conscious again, in my last few hours. I had awakened and graduated. How did it feel? I felt like I had been blasted into the air by a firehose that had love in it, instead of a lot of water.

That's one of the best descriptions yet.
I know it can be hard for anyone to imagine it, but I had become a light being in a lightness world.

Did an angel meet you?
I had been greeted – as I left my body behind – by an angel that had been a guardian angel for all of my life, it said. I asked it if I was dead, and I knew it was going to be a 'yes' answer – and it asked me if that is what I wanted. I said it was, and it gave me the most amazing insight in that moment – that I had become one in the Mind of God again.

Thank you, Lauren. Is there anything you would like to add for those who will read this?
All I could have had or done in my life was healed in its last moment – having lost it, and gained it at the same time. I lost all of my earthly attachments, and gained my earthly graduation, in the healing school of my mind.

"One thing I am convinced of
is that the more you do, the more you can do."

–Lauren Bacall

Clark Gable

Clark Gable died in 1960, at the age of 59. He had dad a heart attack 11 days before, after completing filming of *The Misfits* **with Marilyn Monroe. He was married to Carole Lombard when she died in a plane crash in 1942, at the age of 33. May I speak with Clark?**
I am Clark Gable. How can I be of any assistance in your writing about consciousness?

I do not have any idea how it could be consciousness – if I am conscious of it being conscious also. It could only be conscious if I was not a part of it, meaning how could it be conscious of itself if nothing is outside of it? It could not have any kind of external reference point.

I consider it like having a light on, and asking it, "How dark is it outside?" The light wouldn't have any knowledge of darkness, because it is only lightness. Consciousness would be like lightness – not having any reference for non-consciousness.

I can hear in your mind, "How can there even be non-consciousness?" How can I be conscious of non-consciousness? I can't, because I am like the light that is on, in the analogy of light and consciousness.

Are you saying that we are eternal consciousness?
I am saying that "I am" cannot be "I am not".

"I am" is all I can ever be, including you, and everyone else in the Mind of God. How call all be "I am," and not be all one?

I guess there can only be Oneness, and we 'are' it. I was going to say 'in' it, but it's not possible to be out of it.
Exactly, all Oneness cannot be in parts.

We are Oneness, but as different facets or expressions of it.
All having one thing in common – the 'I am' consciousness.

How would you describe God?
God is the "I am" consciousness, meaning all that is not God, is an illusion.

All that is not kind, loving, or generous is not God, and is an illusion.
An illusion that is not God in your life – dreaming how it can heal into Oneness of 'I am' again. All 'I am' can be is God, and 'All I am not' can only be an illusion.

I understand, and our job is to heal our minds of illusions.
'I am' has no need for healing, but an illusion has only one need – to heal itself. It can only heal itself by dispelling its illusions of 'All I am not'.

How can we best do that?
Allow healing to dispel illusions in your mind by affirming this in every thought – "This is how I – meaning 'I am', dispels illusions. I ask myself – how

can 'I am' conceive of injustice?' I can't – only love is justified.

That's excellent. It will really heal a person's mind, if they keep it in mind.
It heals illusions in a person's mind, making illusions disappear.

They really are magic words, because when a mind heals, and illusions disappear – then a person's life will become an effortless manifestation of their desires.
How could 'I am' not be perfect?

Thank you, Clark. This is some of the most powerful information I have received.
'I am' is all-powerful, meaning it can only be powerful.

I look forward to continuing to heal my mind, and to manifest my desires.
'I am' can be all that you have a desire to be.

I am curious why you had died at the relatively young age of 59.
All that I chased in my life had a lot of "All I am not" illusions in it. How could I keep on chasing illusions if "All I am" has no illusions? I couldn't.

Did an angel meet you when you died?
An angel that had helped me in my life asked me if I decided I could be more than chasing illusions. I said I could, and at that moment, a light in my head illuminated about a million times stronger than the sun – and it had almost pulled me into it before I asked the angel, "How am I going into the light that has..." –

and before I could finish asking, it led me into it by going first, knowing I would follow right along with it.

Did you see your wife, Carole after that?
I came into a lightness atmosphere that I could call heaven, and I encountered all of my departed relatives, and friends I had known in my life.

I then had a projection screening of my life, and I was able to feel what others felt, and hear what they heard in all of my interactions with them. I could have done a lot better than I did in my life.

Thank you, Clark. Would you like to add anything else for people who will read this?
All 'I am' can only be all 'I am' when illusions heal, and disappear from your mind. Plan on it, and life becomes all 'I am' desires, to heal all 'I am' that expresses all that is healed in your mind.

Thank you again, Clark.
I am grateful to you, Mr. Gorman.

"*Honey, we all got to go sometime,
reason or no reason.
Dying's as natural as living.
The man who's too afraid to die
is too afraid to live.*"

–Clark Gable

Carole Lombard

Carole Lombard died in a plane crash in 1942, at the age of 33. The plane crashed into mountains in Nevada, because navigation warning lights were off for wartime blackouts. She was returning from a War Bond tour, and was married to Clark Gable. May I speak with Carole?
Hello, Mr. Gorman. I am Carole.

Hello, Carole. I was reading how saddened that Clark and the country were by your tragic death.
I could have lived a little bit longer, having had that as an option. An angel had given me 2 options in my last moment, as I was exiting my body, before the crash.

Why did you choose to not continue living?
I continued living – I chose not to continue dreaming.

Didn't you have more to do, and more to heal in life?
I did, and I chose not to because I can choose to have them in another lifetime.

What did you experience when you died?
All I could feel was ecstasy in exiting my body. It had been like I couldn't breathe, and then I could – after holding my breath for 1 minute or more. I did not want to hold my breath anymore.

Did your spirit leave your body before the plane crashed?
I heard it crashing, although I didn't realize I had been killed in the plane crash. All I could feel was how ecstatic I was in my new awareness. After I realized I was in the crashed plane, I decided I had to let Clark know I was gone. All I could feel in his mind was the most painful loss I had ever felt. I decided I could only comfort him in my new awareness. In Clark's mind, I had abandoned him in his darkest moment.

Was your lifespan predetermined?
It had been determined in the last moments of my lifetime, and I could have altered it – even after the crash. I could have gone back a few moments to before the crash, where I could choose another lifetime ending.

How would that affect the lifetime endings of everyone else on the plane?
In a dream, allowing other dreamers in it will not affect anyone else's dream. You are only in a dream of your own making.

That's an important topic – that we are individual dreamers, but in a collective dream. Can you describe it?
A collective dream can have as many dreamers in it as it needs for each dreamer to have love, and non-love to choose from in each moment. When a dreamer chooses love, it makes the collective dream heal in the minds of other dreamers – allowing the collective

dream loving instances for its loving dreamer that initiated it.

Wow – that's incredible.
All I hear is how healed your mind is from this information.

In all of my writings, that is one of the main points I would like to convey to people.
Convey it by practicing it. The love in your dream heals in their minds also.

Thank you very much, Carole. Is there anything else that you would like to add?
I am in your dream, healing the collective dream with God's love – the only love there is.

"It is easier to die
when the heart is full of gratitude."

–Carole Lombard

Albert Einstein

Albert Einstein died in 1955, at the age of 76. He collapsed at home, and was taken to the hospital, where he refused surgery to repair a ruptured abdominal artery.

He died peacefully in his sleep shortly after. May I speak with Albert?

Albert Einstein can communicate with Gorman now – although communicating can have its disadvantages, as well as its advantages.

All I can hear is – what are the disadvantages? Albert can detail communications having disadvantages. First, Albert did not find it disadvantageous to have communications, others did. In many communications, they did not understand, and it would have been better to not have communicated at all.

I hear ya – well, I'll try to understand.

Albert hears you, and will try to understand also.

I hear you asking if you need to know quantum physics. The Earth hologram is a quantum particle, having wave properties that are interdependent on what is being observed by you.

It flows in a feedback loop from you, and to you in each moment, appearing as a motion sequence.

That is awesome – each person is the projector of their own universe, which is reflected right back to them in 'the Observer Effect'.

Although it has many observers as individuals, they are only one in a hologram appearing to have motion for unification of its implied separation.

That is very empowering, and sums up our reality very well.

I am hearing in your mind – if there is motion, it is for motioning into stillness back to God.

Well said, but with your words.

All I am doing is describing what you are projecting.

My mantra is that we have a choice every moment – to choose either a godly thought, or an ungodly thought.

Choosing a godly thought – one that is kind, loving, or generous – will create a godly universe for oneself.

It is a healed holographic display that you are projecting.

It also makes us one with God, having no separation in those moments – and as God, we will manifest our desires.

All correct, except for having the incorrect impression that you could ever not be one with God.

Great point. How would you describe our earthly condition?

Allowing life is loving life, meaning it ALL has to be ALLowed to be one with God.

It means we cannot hate, despise, disavow, or 'dis' anything. Our minds will remain peaceful and loving – or at least neutral – to be one with God.

All correct, except being one with God is eternal – not being one is an illusion.

I'd like to hear your answer for this – how can we live the most effectively?

"I am God, and I love all of my holographic projection. I am the only one projecting it."

Affirm it, and it heals in your mind that has an incorrect belief, keeping itself apart from God – which is not conceivable.

I wrote a lot about that in 'The Book of Manifesting', and 'The 4 Secrets of the Universe'. We all know challenging people, and have challenging situations to sometimes deal with. Why did we manifest them in our lives?

The answer is in the question – why did you manifest them in your life?

So that we can allow them? Will that heal the situations, and they go away?

In one word, the answer is "Yes." Nothing happens by chance in the Earth hologram of healing.

On that topic, did you die by 'not allowing' a medical intervention, or were you 'allowing' yourself to die?

I allowed my healing to be in the mental and spiritual bodies – and I allowed my flesh body to have its deadly aneurism.

Although I died, I became one with God – which had never been not one, so I didn't have to do anything but heal my mind – by allowing it to die in this case.

Do you mean the ego mind, left brain, life-mind?

I do, and I can hear in your mind how I am admired for my achievements in academic research. I did not have as much information as I do now in this healed state, but I can give you one insight for your book.

"I am God, and I am all I ever desired for myself – which is you, healing in life on a planet where I can be found in my projection from you."

Thank you, Albert. I love it, and allow it.

How can it not be loved and allowed if it is coming from yourself?

What did you experience when you died?

An angel announced itself as my guardian, and Earth life advisor. Although I had been in a state of delirium, I could hear it very clearly in my mind. It allowed me an opportunity to live, or not – if I chose to not live any longer. I chose not to live any longer, having completed my Lifetime Agreement.

I can hear in your mind, asking what my Lifetime Agreement had been. "Allowing healing is allowing God. How can I be healing if I am God?"

I had a lot to consider in my life, because I was a physicist – but I also had a lot to consider how I came into my life.

I also considered how God could be in the equations I was doing in my research. I know all of the answers now, because I am an aspect of God – but I also know how everything is an illusion of universal proportions.

An illusion is only a perception in my mind. A healed mind has no illusions, or it would not be healed.

What happened when you chose not to continue living?

I almost became God, having no boundaries at all – but I became an 'Albert Einstein aspect of God', bounded by my own limiting thoughts that I am healing.

Was there an explosion of light in your head, that is God?

God had always been in my head; the light had been allowed by my losing my ego mind.

What did you feel?

I felt like I had been blasted into the air, with all of the earthly concerns left behind. "Air" can be 'an intense love for life'. Although air can be hot or cold, it was warm.

What happened after that?

'All I can be' is all I became, as an aspect of God.

Thank you, Albert. What else would you like to say to us, now living in the end of the year, 2025?

Albert can deliver a message for you, and it is from God – although I am God, and you are God. Albert Einstein has one message for humans.

Becoming God is not like being God. It is almost the same, but 'being' God has no needs at all; 'becoming' God has a need to heal itself, in your human logic. 'Allowing' God means that healing is not necessary. Allowing it makes a need for it not necessary.

Be God-like in allowing love, being love, holding love and only love in your mind – and all God can be is all it desired to be – a human being that has nothing it could ever need in its motioning toward being one, in an illusion having everything but one, of God itself.

*"We are slowed down sound and light waves,
a walking bundle of frequencies
tuned into the cosmos.
We are souls dressed up
in biochemical garments,
and our bodies are the instruments
through which our souls play their music."*

—Albert Einstein

Lucille Ball

Lucille Ball died in 1989, from a ruptured abdominal aortic aneurism, one week after a heart valve replacement surgery, in Los Angeles. She was 77 years old. May I speak with Lucy?
I am called 'Lucy', but I am not her anymore. I am an aspect of God, having nothing it needs to be called. 'All I can be', in your terms, is a reflection of your projection, in God's perfection. Nothing in God has an imperfection, meaning I am God's perfection, and so are you.

Thank you, Lucy. Can I call you that?
'All I am' can be called "Lucy," 'All I am not' cannot be called "Lucy" – meaning, yes. Maybe I can call you "Lucy, I am not," – and it still has 'Lucy' in it.

Ha!–I would be called "Lucy", for short.
Okay, "Lucy in a pair of shorts", I can hear how I am making you laugh at the nonsensical conversation.

You made millions of people laugh for decades.
I am a comedienne, not having another career option in my lifetime.

Did you choose to leave the planet when you did?
I already had my checkout instructions when they gave me another heart valve, and another chance to live.

I didn't want another chance to live. I had lived already, and completed my Lifetime Agreements.

Can you tell me what they were?
I agreed I could live and die in an average amount of days, and heal my mind in a comedic episode – not one, a lot of episodes – one for each day. I also agreed that I could heal the minds of others with my comedic episodes, in the early days of television and family situational comedies.

What did you feel when you died?
I felt like 118 pounds of mostly flesh and blood had been instantly turned into light, and I was light. I could not have felt any better than not having a body needing medical attention. Although I didn't have a body, I could hear, and feel, and do anything I allowed myself to hear, feel, and do.

It has been lovely in the light, and 'All I am' has nothing but love for life, and itself. Having love, and only love is being love – meaning I am no longer in a human form. I have no form, only 'All there is' – which is love.

*"Love yourself first
and everything else falls into line.
You really have to love yourself
to get anything done in this world."*

–Lucille Ball

SIGMUND FREUD

Sigmund Freud fled Nazi Germany in 1938, and died of oral cancer in London, in 1939. He was 83, and had been treated for his advanced cancer for years before his death. His physician administered multiple doses of morphine to ease his suffering. May I speak with Sigmund?
'All I am' can be described in one word – "egoless." All I am is a light being, with nothing it needs an ego for.

Your mind has healed into all awareness.
It has actually become an aspect of God that has only one attribute – love.

What is an "aspect of God?"
'All there is' cannot have aspects that are not a part of it. It is not conceivable. All non-love in your perception is an illusion of what I call, "as imaginary as it is temporary."

That's a great way to say it.
I heard it in your mind.

You are considered "the father of psychoanalysis." How do you describe the human mind now?
Humans live in a collective dream, making all they are dreaming illusory.

All have one common goal, and each have their own individual goals – to heal their minds of illusions.

An illusion can heal by allowing its dreamer to know how it is being deceived.

A deception has nothing to gain, except to fool humans into believing their own projections.

What is the truth behind the illusion?
You are God, having a dream that makes it appear you are not. I am also, as well as everyone else.

As God, why do we do that?
All healing has an eternal component in its energy. It offers each individual a glimpse of eternity by healing in life, or in the moment life ends – either, or both. Allow healing and you will be in eternity.

Healing is not necessary in eternity, meaning it is healed. Allowing healing – is allowing eternity – is allowing God.

Individuals healing the illusion have allowed God, and God has healed the individual.

All healing then makes a continuous loop, and eternity illuminates itself – or God illuminates, and the holographic illusion is perpetuated.

All I can hear you asking is, "Why do I feel like I am in a petri dish?"

I can answer it in a few words. All God's healing is in the petri dish. You are not in the dish – you are imagining that you are in the dish to heal.

You are all that is not in the dish, illuminating all that is in the dish.

As you heal, you can see the dish for what it is, from outside of it. At the moment of death, it is clear you are not in the dish.

That's an awesome analogy. What did you feel when you died?
I felt like I became light, as I realized I had never been in the petri dish.

Did you see other light beings?
I did, and all I can describe is an incredible love that cannot be contained. It is 'All there is' – God, and all aspects of God, which are love.

I hear you asking how the dish can be part of 'All there is'. It's not – it is only an illusion in your mind – projected by you, and for you – allowing healing in its illusory sequence of events.

Thank you, Sigmund. How can a person live the most effectively?
Allow healing in your mind by affirming this mantra daily – "I am allowing myself healing in my illusion where I project love – and non-love illusions go away."

That's really great – turn on a light, then darkness doesn't exist.
All darkness heals in lightness, giving it something to illuminate.

"The goal of all life is death."
–Sigmund Freud

William Conrad

William Conrad died of a heart attack in the hospital, in Los Angeles, in 1994. He was 73 years old. May I speak with William?
I am Bill Conrad, although most had known me as 'William', 'the Fatman', or another character like 'Frank Cannon'. How can I be of assistance in your healing journey? I am hearing that I am admired as the 'Marshal Matt Dillon' character in 'Gunsmoke – The Radio Series'.

That's right – I grew up as entertainment dramas had just switched from radio to television, so I only recently discovered Gunsmoke Radio, over 50 years after it had ended in 1961. I think it is a national treasure – superb writing, voice acting, etc.
I enjoyed how it made a lot of people feel, after it had been broadcast.

I can hear in your mind – how did I know how they felt? I always had gotten a lot of feedback and letters – even a marriage proposal, once in a while... not that I didn't get a lot of feedback for being a lot of other things – for my hardheaded devotion to law and order, as an example.

I think radio programs can be far superior to television, because they engage a person's powerful imagination.

I agree, although I did a lot of detective and crime programs, and a few other modern dramas in a television format.

I know how I can help you. I can hear it in my mind. How did I feel in the moment of death? – to be included in your next book. I felt like I had been hit in the chest with a hammer, on the day that I had a heart attack.

I could have died then, but I had one more thing I had to do. I asked God if I could be alive long enough to get help, only because I had dogs that needed to be cared for. Although I had my hardworking wife at home, I had to let her know what happened.

I did not have it in me to give her my heartfelt appreciation for her love and guidance, in my later years. I expected that I could live longer than I did.

Thank you, Bill. Would you like to add anything else?
All becomes God, and God becomes all. All goodness is Godness, allowing all that is not good a place to heal itself in lightness.

Were you met by an angel when you died?
An angel came into my head, in the moment I died. It asked me if I had decided if I wanted to continue on living.

I answered, "How can I continue on living if I died?"

It gave me a choice, and either answer could be healing for me. I did not have much difficulty in choosing, because I could become God-like, or I could become un-God-like in my body again. How difficult a choice is that?

I chose my already expanded awareness as God-like.

What happened next?
I asked the angel, "How come I have a choice after I'm dead?"

It gave an answer I have been considering since then – it said I am God, having a dream of not being God.

I decided I could dream, but never of not being God, ever again. "Not being God, ever again" means I will not be incarnating on the Earth again, although I may incarnate in other locations – but not having a dream of not being God.

How can I heal if I do not dream of not being God? I do not have a healing need, if I don't dream of not being God – although I can be God having a lot of experiences.

Thank you, Bill.
I am God, having an experience of a life-mind acclimating in higher consciousness.

Michelangelo

Michelangelo died in Rome, in 1564, at the age of 88. May I speak with Michelangelo?
I am Michelangelo. Allow me to be of service.

I am writing a book of messages from the spirits of influential people who have died.
Allow me an entry into your book. I can hear you asking me to describe my death moment.

I had thought a lot about death as I sculpted the Pieta, and I had no fear of it, like the Master Jesus in my imagining. I can describe how I died in my lifetime as Michelangelo.

An angel came into my room, after my assistant had gone away. After I acknowledged and accepted the angel there, I had an intense light in my head. All I felt was bliss in my heart, and my mind – and I didn't feel my body. I had died at that moment.

I hear you asking if I had gone away with the angel. I did go away, but it was not in another place, it was everywhere.

Did you meet God?
I did, and how can I best explain that I am God, and I imagined that I was not God for my entire life. All I can describe is – I dreamed I am not God, and at my death I awakened in God.

I was never not God, but I dreamed I was.

Michelangelo has another insight to share. I can never be 'not God', and I can never not be you. We are one in God and as God, imagining having infinite degrees of separation.

I can hear you asking – are we supposed to heal the separation? All Oneness has no separation to heal – only your imagining it. Imagining it can be healed by not imagining it. How can it not be imagined?

All degrees of separation can be imagined in one point, in the center of your mind. It is then imagined as having one point of reference in your mind, and it can only be projected from there.

If an incident has you concerned, ask it how it could be outside of you. It will always answer the same answer –

"I am not outside of you. It is your imagination projecting it out."

Although it appears as an incident outside of you, it had only been an imaginary instance, for you to heal it back into its point of reference – the center point of your mind.

Conversely, I could also project out what I desire in life.
It can be healed in your mind, and projected from your heart.

How do we heal it, and project it?

Imagine it, because it is an imaginary instance in your dream of life. Heal it by loving all of its desired effects in your dream of life.

Next, it is placed in the heart chamber having the Heart Master Flower of Life.

After the healed desire is placed in the Flower of Life, ask it to heal into your life. Although it may not give you an answer right away, imagine it as blue-magenta lightness projecting out, and illuminating the entire universe.

It heals into life, as you had projected it to.

Thank you, Michelangelo. That matches what I have been discovering. The blue-magenta light is the Light of God Mind, at the center of our Earth hologram, and it comes through our DNA portals that we have opened.

All correct – in a hologram of light, have no illusions about healing it in lightness. All having non-light will not exist in the lightness.

"Do not fret,
for God did not create us to abandon us."

–Michelangelo

Frank Lloyd Wright

Frank Lloyd Wright died in 1959, at the age of 91. He died in Phoenix, Arizona from complications following surgery for an intestinal obstruction. May I speak with Frank?
I am Frank Lloyd Wright. Gorman can communicate his thoughts, and I can hear him.

I can also communicate my thoughts to him, although I can hear him before he asks me anything.

Hello, Frank. You were America's most well-known architect in your lifetime, and still today, 67 years after you passed away.
All I can hear in your mind is how you loved that my designs were organically created, flowing from nature.

All I had in mind was creating extensions of natural forms, and how they are always functional.

Your works, almost all residences, are mostly historical landmarks now.
All I hear in your mind is if I have any input for your architectural career. All creativity has one, and only one thing in common – God, its creative force for expressing creation through you, and everyone else.

God is in all of nature, having instilled itself in it, allowing itself a home. God having a home in all of nature means that I cannot improve on it, only extend it. All having a home in nature, also happens to be beautiful.

One thing I learned from channeling information about our reality is that 90-degree angles are not natural or flowing, and create fear on a subtle energy level. Most of our building spaces and rooms are composed of 90-degree angles.

An angle of 60 degrees induces God Mind.

Correct, like a hexagonal honeycomb in a beehive, each side is 60 degrees from the center.

All beehives have instilled God Mind into the bees. Instilling God Mind can be accomplished in another way for humans.

I hear in your mind saying, "Let's hear it."

All angles can be added together in a series, totaling in one number that has God Mind as an attribute. It would be a number having a multiple of 60, and it could be a Fibonacci number of mathematical proportions.

I just drew a diagonal line across a square, from one corner to the opposite corner. That created 2 triangles, with angles of 90, 45, and 45 degrees – totaling 180 degrees, and multiple of 3 times 60. I then offset the 2 triangles to change the square into a more interesting shape – possibly with more beneficial angles.

It is a design in my glass window patterns.

I would like to ask you about your death. What was it like?
I could have lived a little bit longer, but I decided not to. I had completed my Lifetime Agreements, and I can tell you what they were.

First, I agreed that healing had to be my most important achievement in life, and it was. My life had a number of tragedies that I had to accept, and to heal.

My next agreement was to be a creative influence on others. I did a lot in that area also – and my last agreement came to me on my deathbed.

I decided I could live as a God-like energy in the minds of all having creative pursuits, if I am asked for assistance.

I am always actively assisting in your designs for people.

Thank you very much.
I know how proficient you are in designing buildings, and drawing them in an easy-to-understand presentation.

Did an angel greet you when you died?
An angel had greeted me in my hospital room, and discussed my first two agreements, adding a third one.

All I hear in your mind is if it was my guardian angel. It had been my guardian angel in life, and is no longer around me because my life is completed.

Thank you very much, Frank – for your contributions to architecture, and for continuing to help and inspire others.
Is there anything you would like to say to people now?
I am a God – like energy that has endless creativity in eternity. I am activating it in your mind if you allow me, and ask me to.

"Study nature, love nature,
stay close to nature.
It will never fail you."

–Frank Lloyd Wright

GEORGE ORWELL

George Orwell died of tuberculosis in 1950, at the age of 46. He is known for his books '1984', and 'Animal Farm'. Shortly before his death, he married his second wife in his hospital room. May I speak with George?
George Orwell, as I had been known, is here in your communication. How may I help you?

Your books warned of authoritarian control and censorship, and you coined the terms 'double-speak', 'group think', and 'thought crimes'. It is clear that we are building a total control grid, and when digital currencies are required to do business, there will be no freedom left. Behavior will be controlled.
It is all here, as I had written about.

How did you know it was coming?
Almost exactly as you are doing – I accessed higher consciousness, and got information.

I read that your book, 1984, is the most banned book in history. It describes our dystopian future. The controllers don't ever want the truth being told.
It cannot be concealed forever. It is always the same – authoritarian controllers lose their control, and the individual finds freedom from tyranny – although a lot of people lose their lives in the process.

It is late 2025 now – are we heading into a period of digital tyranny, and mass death?
In the next 4 ½ years, the currency collapse destroys human productivity, and peoples' wealth. Allowing it heals it – meaning, how can it be stopped? It cannot be, because in your society, a large percentage of the population doesn't care.

Mind control and mass brainwashing are very effective now also.
I can detail how it is deployed in the media, and in other invisible ways.

What are the invisible ways?
All having an internet connecting device are being constantly immersed in an invisible frequency that can modify all of their thoughts. It can also install new beliefs into their minds.

It obviously affects a lot of people – why not others?
A belief has to be accepted for it to have a detrimental effect on a person.

This book is about death, and life after death – which may be coming sooner than a lot of people expect. What did you experience when you died?
A devil named 'Lucifer' called my name, and I did not respond to it. Then my guardian angel got in front of it. All devils cannot be in any lightness. Actually, it hurts them immensely. All Lucifer had in mind was how much evil was in my book, 1984.

I had several conversations with Lucifer, in my book *The 4 Secrets of the Universe*. Lucifer said that the devils are not evil, but they are attracted to it – and it is only in human minds.
Ha, ha – I like that interpretation of evil.

What I say is that when you have kind, loving, and generous thoughts – you are one with God Mind. There is no separation, and God expresses itself as you in those moments.
Having all kind, loving, and generous thoughts can make you become God-like in manifesting your desires – all detailed in your book, 'The Book of Manifesting'.

"Nothing in nature hates life, or itself – only humans" is a point from the book that I like.

So, you have uploaded my books?
Accessing the healing information, yes.

Did you motion away from the Earth with your guardian angel?
I did, and I have not been around earth since I died – except I have been mentioned in many conversations about the future, which has arrived.

Thank you, George. Is there anything that you would like to say to humanity now?
All evil is only in your mind. Allow in only God Mind, and evil cannot exist.

"The further a society drifts from truth, the more it will hate those who speak it."

"The most effective way to destroy people is to deny and obliterate their own understanding of their history."

"All tyrannies rule through fraud and force, but once the fraud is exposed, they must rely exclusively on force."

"The people will believe what the media tells them to believe."

"Some ideas are so stupid that only intellectuals believe them."

"However much you deny the truth, the truth goes on existing."

"Real power is achieved when the ruling class controls the material essentials of life, granting them and *withholding them from the messes as if they were privileges."*

"A generation of the unteachable is hanging upon us like a necklace of corpses."

"Journalism is printing what someone else does not want printed; everything else is public relations."

"We know that no one ever seizes power with the intention of relinquishing it."

"If liberty means anything at all, it means the right to tell people what they do not want to hear."

–George Orwell

Linda McCartney

Linda McCartney died from breast cancer in 1998, at the age of 56. She died in Tucson, Arizona, and had gone horseback riding the day before. It was decided to not let her know the full extent of her illness. May I speak with Linda?
'Allabalong' was my favorite recipe. I know my recipes had caught your interest.

Yes, they did.
Allabalong is made with love, having nothing else in it for enlightenment. Allabalong can be made, or eaten in a lot of different preparations.

What is it?
Allabalong has only one ingredient – 'All that belongs', and 'All' is God's love.

I'll use it in everything.
Allabalong is 'All there is', so it only has to be appreciated in everything.

Can you please tell me what it was like when you died?
All I could hear in my mind was an angel asking me if I could meet with it in the most loving, healed place there is.

All I could hear in my mind was myself saying, "Yes" – and in that moment, an intense light had enveloped me. In the light was an angel.

"Hello, Linda. I am glad you have arrived. I had been expecting you.

Nothing had been more anticipated than greeting you on your arrival.

'Greeting' has a new meaning, because I have always been with you.

Allow me an opportunity to acquaint you with God Mind, which is nothing more or less than your mind.

'All it can be' has never been more complete than it is now, having awakened its aspect of Linda.

All I can do is facilitate 'All that is' to become all that it can be. It does not make sense, but it has aspects that are asleep, believing they are not 'All there is'."

After I heard it, I could understand everything, and I knew that I was one with everything.

Thank you, Linda. Did you go with the angel, away from the Earth?
All having an earthly connotation is an illusion. All having an eternal connotation is God Mind, and is 'All there is'.

What would you like to say to people now?
'All I can be' cannot be any more or less. I am God Mind's aspect of Linda Eastman, believing I had been an

animal – human being – but I only dreamed that I was. Linda Eastman can become anything I desire, but it can only be in a dream to heal myself – and it cannot be without a limit on its duration.

That describes our dream of a life, in the Earth hologram.
A hologram is one whole in each of its light pixels. Each can influence the whole, but not be more than the whole.

I can hear in your mind – how can it influence the whole? It can in the Earth hologram because it is an inversion of itself – meaning each pixel projects it.

Is each person a pixel?
Each pixel is a living person, but each living person is not a pixel. I can explain how it is true.

If a person has negative or antagonistic attitudes or beliefs, then all they can do has nothing to do with illuminating the hologram.

If a person has a loving and positive attitude, then they influence all of the Earth hologram pixels.

That is very profound. Can you please give me a practical example?
I can, although it may be a bit personal from my experience. All I can describe is from my marriage to Paul McCartney, and having him as an example of how it can be done. In his belief system, there is nothing negative about it.

His positive mindset has each pixel in the Earth hologram instructed by him. Nothing in his Earth hologram is going to be against him.

If someone is negative, what happens?

All of the Earth hologram pixels will not be in an organization favoring them.

It's a self-perpetuating feedback loop.
A loop has no ending – it just keeps going around. It can also be called 'a self-fulfilling negative loop'.

Can you give me an affirmation to remember?
"All in my Earth hologram has only love from me. All in my Earth hologram has only love for me."

I will practice being positive.
"My Earth hologram has all positive pixels, allowing my hologram to illuminate my healed desires."

Thank you, Linda.
All is light. I can illuminate your desires to heal them in the light, if you ask me to.

"Oppression won't win, the light comes from within."
–Linda McCartney

Cleopatra

Cleopatra had acclimated to my mind when I was writing her spirit messages in my recent book, *The Moment of Death*. She asked if she could stay with me, in my mind. It was several months ago. Cleopatra, are you still with me?

I am – how can I describe my experience being in your mind? I am acclimating in it right now, and I can become an architect in the 21st century. I am also a dog owner, and love preparing a lot of healthy meals for myself, and the dogs. I am an avid defender of all that is fair. I also like absurdities, and see a lot of them.

You are describing me pretty well. I also like writing spiritual messages, and to see things from the soul's perspective.

I was going to include more in my description about how I am in contact, because I am in your mind – and your mind is not in its earthly orientation, making interactions mostly disappointing.

Hey, I don't think that's necessarily because of me.

I can describe it from my perspective. All I can describe is how, in your mind, you have been programmed to be a giver. Being a giver makes everyone else a receiver, although they are not appreciative in most instances.

Which makes it an unfair, or unbalanced exchange of energy.

It is allowed, making it agreed upon that nothing is expected in return for your giving.

Nothing is expected in return from your relationships, but in a hologram, you only have one relationship – in a relationship with only yourself. In this individual relationship, it is only necessary to appreciate yourself.

In appreciation of yourself, all in the hologram is appreciative of you also. It can be no other way in the love hologram.

I guess that if I feel unappreciated, it will turn off appreciation in my hologram.
All a hologram can be is a lightness having its input coming from a lightness in yourself.

All darkness is not an input, it is just darkness. In a hologram having a little darkness, illuminate it in yourself, and it will become lightness in your hologram.

How can I do that?
In an instance of not being appreciated, or remembering how you were not appreciated – accept having been unappreciated, allowing it an instance of appreciation for giving you a lesson in giving, and not receiving.

If I have a disappointing thought, should I thank it for giving me a lesson?
All giving can only be in your mind, and only to yourself. Allow all disappointing instances of giving,

acceptance for what they gave you – a lesson in giving, and not expecting anything in return.

If you do not expect anything in exchange for giving, you cannot be disappointed.

Great point.
In a hologram of light, it will only illuminate in giving, and not be darkened in disappointment – meaning, always appreciate all that you are giving away, because it is light, and illuminating all in your hologram.

That will have a significant impact on my reality.
In a hologram of giving, it has only one impact – giving in exchange for nothing means it will have to find something to give you in an exchange of energy.

Go on...
In an exchange of energy, it can only increase because it is in a hologram of infinite expression – meaning, it cannot be limited in exchanging for what it is you desire.

Wow, wow, wow.
All giving is always by you, and for you.

I have always believed – and seen it – that my giving comes right back to me, 10 times over.
It is a belief that has defined your hologram, allowing all of the hologram to heal in its receiving, and gift back to you in multiples of 10.

When I give, I will see it as an input to my own hologram that has generosity as an operating principle. I will never be disappointed by not receiving appreciation just because it's unseen, because that's not true.

It illuminates the entire hologram, meaning its illumination is all that's being seen.

Thank you, Cleopatra. This changes everything for me.

I am elated, and I know how you feel because I am in your mind.

"Giving" could be with money to someone in need, food to the birds, time and attention to someone who needs support, or just a smile and kind words to someone who is not expecting them.

All of them can be given freely, and not impact your life – except in a positive way.

Go on – I like talking about what impacts my life in a positive way.

A giving person is the receiving person in a hologram with one giver, and one receiver – with many gifts he has been given.

All of his gifts were given, with nothing expected in return – except to heal himself.

Healing himself in a hologram has only one direction – it is outward, but in an illusion, it is only inward. All heals inward, which then heals outward, and so on.

What we put out is what we'll get back.

All is an input needing an output – so, it it only for you, because it is from you. In a hologram of life on Earth, input equals output – meaning, how could it be any other way in a program for healing itself?

Here is a poem from my book, *The Lightness of Being'*

Your Gift

It's clear to me
   each person is unique
and signed up for life
   where they wanted to be

to discover their gifts
   always God-given
and to share them with others
   openly or hidden

and also to learn
   how to discern
some gifts are endowed
   and others are earned

You will always receive
   what you have allowed
and in what you believe
   which brings me to how

the only wealth
   is in what you give away
and the way to health
   is in what you say

to yourself
 and to me in a way
that you're glad you received
 my gifts to display

by celebrating life
 from day to day
and in what you achieve
 come what may

adding love to life
 and love to your soul
which gifts back to me
 making us whole

[thank you for sharing
 you gave me a lift
and all of life
 has received your gift]

"And make death proud to take us."

−Cleopatra

Elizabeth Taylor

Elizabeth Taylor died of heart failure in 2011, at age 79, while at Cedars-Sinai Medical Center in Los Angeles. May I speak with Elizabeth?
I am Liz. Can I be any more informal than that?

Hello, Liz. Do you know why I contacted you, or did you contact me first?
I had already known you were going to communicate with me, so I notified you of my availability.

Are there periods when you are not available?
I am always everywhere, making me always available.

I just spoke with Linda McCartney about the Earth hologram. She said something really important – "If a person has negative or antagonistic attitudes or beliefs, then all they can do has nothing to do with illuminating the hologram. If a person has a loving and positive attitude, then they influence all of the Earth hologram pixels."

Let's talk about influencing all of the Earth hologram pixels
All having any light in it is in the Earth hologram. If a person has a negative thought, it is not illuminating – and if a person has a positive one, it illuminates the entire hologram. If it illuminates the entire hologram, it will be the illumination of your thought.

Will positive thoughts manifest in reality, or does a person have to have positive beliefs?

Love is what illuminates the hologram. All loving, kind, and generous thoughts illuminate the entire hologram. Healed thoughts are in the hologram, and will manifest in reality. I can hear in your mind asking if there is a shortcut to manifesting. No. I can hear you asking for us to make one. I do not know if it is possible to make a shortcut, but impatience could make a short circuit.

You are right. Can you tell me your experience when you died?

I can also give you a shortcut for dying, if you want one – I am joking.

All I could feel was myself leaving my body – out of the top of my head, into a lightness brighter than looking at a million suns. An angel had come into my awareness, and it gave me a big, "Hello".

I didn't have any idea what it was, so I didn't answer it. In that instant, it gave me an insight for me to know where I am, and who it was. I became all I had been before I was born – an aspect of God having all awareness in my mind, and in my soul.

It could not be any other way, because I am an aspect of God that had been dreaming I was not.

Did the angel give you the option to go back in time, and not have heart failure – to continue living?

It gave me a few options: I could continue on with it into even greater lightness. Although I had other options, I wanted it.

Another option was to go into a timelessness, and re-enter my life a few moments before my heart failure, and continue living my life. Although I had died, I did not want to go back and live any longer.

The next option had me confused, because it said that I could have both of the first two options together.

It then held my hand, and gave me a preview of my two options together.

In a final moment of life, my heart had stopped, and I could be in both options at the same moment – in a moment before death, and also in an eternal moment in the Mind of God. I did not have any interest in being in a coma, although I did like being in an eternal moment in the Mind of God.

I agreed on the first option, and had gone into even greater lightness. In the lightness, I met God.

God gave me an interesting welcome by being my exact likeness, although I know it had to be more than that.

I then had an incredible insight – that it was me, and I was more than that.

How could I not have known I was God? I should have, but no one really explained it very well – although I did learn a lot about an eternal life.

Thank you, Liz. That was very interesting. Your explanation should help those who read this to understand.

All God can be is all 'I am' – meaning I am you, and I am me.

"Follow your passions,
follow your heart,
and the things you need will come."

–Elizabeth Taylor

Steve Jobs

Steve Jobs died from pancreatic cancer, at the age of 56. He was diagnosed in 2003, and had a liver transplant in 2009. The cancer spread, and he died peacefully at home in 2011. May I speak with Steve?
I can already hear in your mind if my cancer treatments helped me, or hurt me. I had cancer that I invited to heal in my mind, and only in my mind.

What was the cancer?
I had a belief for most of my life that I could not be inventive enough in my mind, having nothing in it inventive at all.

It appears that you were extremely inventive, and your products are used by millions, if not billions of people.
I admit that I overcompensated for my lack of inventiveness.

Your business partner was extremely inventive, but I read that you hold over 450 patents.
If one had a cure for cancer, it could be my most important one.

What is the cure for cancer?
All cancers have one common denominator – a lie in your mind that has become a cancer in your body.

How can we heal all the lies, especially if we don't know what they are?
Affirming a truth can negate the lies – "Here lies my lies. Although I held onto them, I now hold them in the light of truth, and every lie has died."

That's really good. I am writing about the death experience. Can you tell me what it was like?
I enjoyed it, mainly because I was on pain-killing medications, and also because I had an awesome experience in my already expanded awareness. I was loved completely, and in my awareness, I knew I was God having a life where I had not been aware of my 'God in a lifetime dream' mode of operation.

What did you experience?
All I can describe has a lot of interesting details that cannot be fully described. All have a lot in common with my trips on LSD, although dying is a lot more love-encompassing. If I had known, I would have died a lot sooner.

It occurred to me recently that people who read my books might see dying as more appealing than living.
It is healing, so it is. All deaths have one common denominator – it defeats a life, but it completely liberates a person's eternal spirit. All have another common denominator – they heal the mind in an awakening in all awareness and love.

Did an angel meet with you before you died?
It did – it came into my room where I had been in bed for my last days. It came into my room 5 times.

In the first visit, it asked me if I knew about angels visiting people. I said I did not, except for in a few spiritual and religious texts.

In the next angel meeting, it came into my room, and asked me if I knew why it had come to visit me. I did not answer it right away, but it knew what I thought – that I could be dying in the near future.

In the third visit, it gave me information I needed to decide on whether I should leave, or not. After I decided I could leave in the near future, it gave me another few days to be with my family.

In the fourth visit, it came into my head while I was sleeping. It asked me if I could go into my body one last time, so I could close it down in an orderly manner – not unlike a computer in its shutting down process.

In its fifth and final visit, I had been wondering if it was coming back, and it appeared in front of my face, only about a foot and a half away from me. It asked me if that was going to be my last day, and I acknowledged that it was. In the instant I had the thought, an intense light came into my head, and I started to be pulled into it, without my body.

I could see and hear everything in my new awareness. I loved how I felt, and am feeling. All I could have been in life, I am in my afterlife, because I am not limited anymore. In my all-aware and unlimited state, I am God having been in a dream of awakening in life – and being all awake in losing my life.

What are the best cures to heal cancerous cells in the body – other than healing the mind?
A cancer has many anti-cancer compounds to kill cancer cells. An anti-cancer compound has ill effects on cancer cells, and not on healthy cells. The most important one has been in use for thousands of years – Frankincense. It kills cancer cells in the body.

Another anti-cancer compound is capsaicin in different peppers. It kills cancer cells. Another cancer-curing treatment is alkalizing the body by ingesting all vegetables and legumes. Blueberries are alkalizing, and can heal malignancies.

All of the cancer-curing treatments that I mentioned can be combined for more robust effectiveness. Getting an energetic healing adjustment will also work, as you have demonstrated. Nothing heals faster than healing in the mind, which can be instantaneous.

Thank you very much, Steve. What would you like to say to people now?
If I could live my life again, I would live it without the gadgets and devices – intended for making life easier, and people more connected than ever. It can also cause a lot of adolescents to disengage, in their most important years to become engaged.

Tell me something I don't know about cancer. I wrote about those topics in my books, *The 4 Secrets of the Universe*, and, *The 5th Secret – In the Universe that I Am*.
All cancers can be eliminated by affirming the mantra I had given in the beginning of this communication,

although cancer can be an excuse to die in a delayed period of time. Death is inevitable in everyone's life – it depends how you choose to end it.

Life doesn't really end – it reverts to its original form of expanded awareness, and incredible lovingness in the Mind of God.

A theme of my books, *All About the Soul's Journey*, and *The Moment of Death*, is that we always have choices – before being born, during our lifetimes, before our deaths – and even after our deaths.

Actually, life is never choice-less, and each choice can be a healing choice, or not. The first choice is always in your mind, and it is accepted, and creates a new universe for you. All choices are healing choices, because unhealed choices will heal in death. All choices have love to be chosen for healing yourself. Love for yourself – and how you love yourself – is creating the new universe you are going to live in.

Do each of us create a new universe for ourselves in every moment?

Each new moment is all moments because there is only one moment in the Mind of God – and it copies itself every moment, depending on your choices.

When we choose loving thoughts–about ourselves and others – we are not separated from God, which then creates the universe of our desires.

All creation is created in love, so it cannot be any other way in the love hologram.

All evil is not in the Mind of God, so is therefore an illusion in our world of opposites.
In a dream of love and non-love, it has to be in it as a darkness prop for healing in your mind – and healing can only be in your mind.

What can we do to heal our minds of all the "darkness props" that are always trying to get our attention?
Affirming this heals all darkness props in your mind – "I am allowing darkness in my dream, only because I can illuminate it in my mind. I allow it. I illuminate it in my mind with healing thoughts for all involved, and I love myself for healing it in my mind – because it only needs to heal in my mind. I am one with God Mind – all non-love is inconceivable in my universe."

That's not really denying it, it is allowing it and healing it – which is all we can do, or need to do. I wrote a lot about that in *The Book of Manifesting*.
All in life has one purpose – for you to heal all of it in your mind. Healing it in your mind by allowing it has only one effect – it creates a healed universe for yourself.

Thank you, Steve. I have a lot of opportunities to practice with. I understand that as my mind heals, the "non-love opportunities to practice with" will go away.
All heal in your mind, meaning you no longer need them in your life. Healing has only one direction – it comes from you, and in coming from you, it cannot be

going anywhere in an illusion of time and space. It is coming to you, meaning it never left. Although it never left, healing illuminates your entire hologram.

Wow – that's a lot of great information that people can use to heal their minds, and live more effectively – and manifest their dreams.

All heals in love, so live what you love, and love will illuminate your entire hologram.

"*Focus and simplicity...
once you get there,
you can move mountains.*"

–Steve Jobs

Message from God Mind

May I speak with someone who has died, but then chose to skip back in time, and avoided that particular death?
All can have that experience in their lives if they choose it. It happens often and unconsciously for most people.

Because death is such a welcome relief, it seems that most of those experiences would result in the person choosing dying over living.
All have chosen death in their last moment on Earth, and not reentering their body. All having an assignment on Earth choose not to leave before it is completed.

Is it a personal challenge to complete the Lifetime Agreements?
It could be more than one lifetime for the necessary skills to be developed, but yes. Having more than one agreement to complete is the other challenge.

How is it that a person can skip back in time, and avoid an outcome that has already happened?
An illusion has one thing in it for it to be accepted as not an illusion. In your earthly lifetime, each moment is arranged in a timeline that never ends. That is absurd that it has no ending, but it is accepted that it had a beginning.

How could it ever have begun if it has no ending? All it has is a point of beginning, and no ending. It never ends, so how could it have begun? It never did begin, meaning it cannot end if it never began. Now it makes more sense because the illusion has no beginning or ending – it has one moment in which it is playing over and over.

In its endless moment of playing over and over, it is possible for one in timelessness to enter into the illusion in any moment. In the case of one who has died, it means they have to go into the moment before death, and choose another outcome.

Thank you for that explanation. There is always only one present moment. If I make it loving and peaceful in my mind, how does it influence future moments – or are there future moments?

A moment is only in the instant it becomes another moment in the next instant. In that moment, it copies the entire holographic universe instantly, becoming the next moment in time. It copies all you are illuminating in it.

Love is what illuminates it. All love illuminating in the hologram will illuminate in its new copies. Darkness only has a place in it where it is not illuminated – in your mind.

Is it possible to not have darkness, or non-love in our holograms?

It can be done if you love everything in your hologram. Everything in a hologram is illuminated by love, making everything in it love. Non-love is a call for love. It can be loved, and it heals in unseen ways.

That gives me a new perspective – everything is love, or is in need of love. Love can be my only response, either way.
Loving responses create a new loving universe every moment.

And I will live in a new loving universe.
A holographic universe of love, illuminating your desires in the Mind of God, allowing them to manifest in reality.

I love that.
Allow it to become a new holographic universe every moment.

Peter Sellers

Peter Sellers died of a heart attack at the age of 54, in 1980.
He had just returned to London that day, and visited the crematorium site of his parent's ashes for the first time.
May I speak with Peter?
All Chance has to say is, "I like to watch."

That's a funny line from your movie, *Being There*. The outtakes at the end are hilarious.
Hello Gorman, I did not have a meeting scheduled, did I?

No.
How could I be in a meeting if it had not been scheduled?

Let's ask Inspector Clouseau.
I see – I must have lost my appointment book with your appointment in it.

I must get another one after our appointment, and put it in it.

Yes, I see.
I am investigating how I might have died of a heart attack, because I am alive, and have been accused of murdering myself.

We'll get to the bottom of it. I will be the investigator, and ask you a series of questions. Why did you have a heart attack?

I had been in a life having little, or no love in it. I mean, love for myself – others loved me, but I didn't.

Was your lifespan predetermined?
I had a Lifetime Agreement for not living into old age.

What was your main Lifetime Agreement?
"All having a laugh allow healing in their minds. Agree to healing people in making them laugh. All heals in laughter."

Did an angel greet you when you died?
An angel advised me before I died, although I did not know I was going to be dying soon. It advised me about having love for myself, because that is what I am. I did not allow myself to love myself, because I didn't allow a lot in my life as Peter Sellers. It also did not help any of my marriages, I admit.

I can hear you asking if the angel met me after I died. A lot of angels had met me in the moment I arrived in a lightness I cannot describe – other than having a light be so bright, it is not a light anymore–and everything in it is the entire universe illuminating itself.

Now I am able to discern what is God, and what is not God. Everything is God, and not-God is everything I had to control – my fears, and my intolerance. How do I know all of this? I am God, as I had been describing – and I do not fear anything, or not tolerate anything.

How can I apologize for my intolerance to other people? By forgiving myself for my actions, because we are all one in the light I had been describing. I had been hurting only myself in my actions, in my life.

My understanding is that our non-loving actions do not exist because they are not in the light of God – they are shadows that are not illuminated or healed as you forgive yourself.
All correct, except my actions had a lasting impact on everyone else. All being one is fine, but how can one be in conflict with anything if it is the only one? It cannot be in conflict, except in a human mind, healing itself of conflicting ego demands. Nothing in life heals like loving yourself enough to forgive yourself.

Thank you, Peter.
All I can be is lightness in the lightness – I am part of all that is.

"It won't be easy, that is why I have always failed where others have succeeded."

−Peter Sellers

Florence Nightingale

Florence Nightingale died in 1910, at the age of 90. She died peacefully in her sleep, at home in London. Florence was an English social reformer, statistician, and the founder of modern nursing. May I speak with Florence?
A "Hello" has been going out to you to hear me for a number of days in your earthly timeline.

Hello, Florence.
I can hear you in your mind, admiring me for my contributions to humanity, in regards to healing.

You said that you were trying to get my attention?
I did get it, and now I'm going to give you my accounting of how I did all that I did, in a society of men having leadership roles – except for a Queen figurehead.

I accomplished a lot by first not having a husband. Although I had companions, I did not need a husband to look after. I had a lot of other people who needed looking after. I am most well-known for my looking after, and it became the practice of nursing.

You made significant contributions to humanity, and to ease peoples' suffering.
I did all I could do in my capacity. All in my capacity is in everyone's capacity, I imagined.

How could it not be in everyone's capacity to care for others in need? I could not fathom it.

I could have had an easy life, but life is never that easy.

What do you think of our medical establishment today?
It can be a lot better in many areas, especially in curing illnesses.

I think the intention is to manage them, rather than to cure them.
And in some cases, it created them.

I know, we recently had a global pandemic from a manmade virus.
Achieving little in the way of depopulation, as it was intended- though it has made a lot of females infertile by giving them injections intended for that purpose.

It was a diabolical plan, and it was somewhat successful- with no one held accountable.
Achievement in life means how much can be stolen from others, in many advanced societies – including their lives.

All governments have been collaborating on how to achieve a net reduction in global population numbers.

I'd like to see a reduction in governments.
A government can impose its directives by force – you cannot.

In my book, *The 4 Secrets of the Universe*, I wrote a chapter 'Only One Antidote'. it

describes how Ivermectin will heal cells and organs by undoing the effects of mRNA shots.

Achievement in life means how much can be gifted from your heart in generosity.

Also in *The 4 Secrets of the Universe*, I asked if there are too many people on the Earth. The answer was, "Not too many people, too many dissatisfied people." This is attributed to the rise of mass media broadcasts in the last 2-3 generations – where people see what they don't have, and they want it. They become envious of others, and dissatisfied with their own lives – not to mention that they are being very effectively programmed and manipulated.

Achievement in life means how much can be stolen from others, including their happiness.

I wrote about the End Times, social upheaval, financial collapse, a catastrophic pole shift, etc. – and wanted to move someplace safe. I have decided that the only peaceful place can be in my mind, and the future will be the future that I create. I will die when I'm ready to die. We all signed up for this collective dream.

Achievement in life means having a healed mind, and you may not be tested if you are prepared.

That's what I meant about the future being what I create. It will magically change, depending on what I fear – or what I love. Fear and love will close and open portals in our DNA. Open portals are open to the light of God

Mind on the other side, meaning we are one, and no longer separated from God.
It is magically changing now, in your writing this book.

How so?
This can be a book in demand for a long time – I know it.

Can you please tell me about your death experience?
Achievement in life means having a nice and peaceful transition out of it. I had mine, and I had a magnificent journey into healing and love.

Were you greeted by an angel before you died?
I was, and I hadn't met an angel before then, even though it said it had always been near me.

What else did the angel say?
It also declared my hands had been healing instruments, and mattered more than medical instruments.

Did you see the angel in your room, or was it in your mind?
It came into my room, in the corner up high, illuminating in lightness.

What did it look like?
It looked like all angels had been depicted – beautiful and having no gender, although it was a bit feminine.

It had flowing garments, and a large set of wings.

Did it introduce itself?

It did give a greeting in my mind. It already had my name, and seemed to know all about me.

I couldn't believe it when it made it known how many defeated people I had saved in my life.

I am grateful for having the opportunity to help all of them, meaning I'm grateful that I could even help them.

How many times did the angel visit you?
It came only once, because I left in that visit. It healed me in the most magnificent way, as I left my body, into the light.

Next, it gave me an introduction to the next healing parts of my eternal life. I entered into an auditorium, and all of my lifetime interactions had been illuminating on a large white panel of some kind. I felt and heard what others felt and heard in those interactions. I could not have been better in some, and I could not have been worse in others.

I could hear and feel how I could have been a better person.

Why do you think we incarnate to learn how to be better people?
I can answer it easily from my perspective. Each of us is God in a non-loving dream that we had chosen for healing ourselves in.

In the dream, the goal is to awaken by healing the mind of its dreaming how it is not one with everything.

That is not even possible, for you or anything else that is a God aspect – to not be one in the Mind of God.

Thank you, Florence. What would you like to say to people now?

I am Florence Nightingale. Call on me and I will heal you in hundreds of little ways that add up to one big way – "one" being its significance.

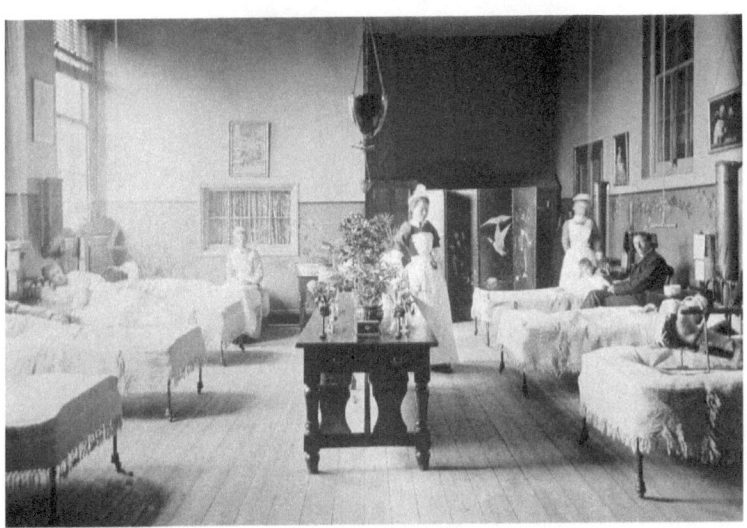

*"A nurse will always give us hope,
an angel with a stethoscope."*

"Never underestimate the healing effects of beauty."

*"I attribute my success to this:
I never gave or took any excuse."*

*"The very first requirement in a hospital
is that it should do the sick no harm."*

—Florence Nightingale

Afterword

I've been seeing a particular star lately that is twinkling, and others are not. Can I communicate with the star?
It always has a lightness message for you.

Is it specifically for me?
It aligns with you in its twinkling, only for it to be heard and seen by you.

What does it want me to hear?
"All can become an enemy or a friend; it depends how it was allowed in your holographic projection."

Do all of the stars have messages?
All have illumination in your DNA, in the inside-out universe always inside of you – projecting out in a hologram.

Affirmations

"All I have is my power, and my angelic guidance. I direct my mind, my heart, and my courage to hear them only."

—Margaret Hamilton

"I am God, and I have no needs. I am healed, and the universe grants my healed wishes."

—Dean Martin

"All I am is all I am ever going to be – an aspect of God having healing needs in my mind. Allow my mind to heal in its love for itself, having no forgiveness needs to heal. Allow my love, having no healing needs, a home in my mind."

—John Wayne

"My mind is peaceful. Love has a home in my mind. I do not need anything, and have no need for forgiveness."

—Paul Gorman

"I am God, and I love all of my holographic projection. I am the only one projecting it."

—Albert Einstein

"I am God, and I am all I ever desired for myself – which is you, healing in life on a planet where I can be found in my projection from you."

—Albert Einstein

"I am allowing myself healing in my illusion where I project love – and non-love illusions go away."

–Sigmund Freud

"All in my Earth hologram has only love from me. All in my Earth hologram has only love for me."

–Linda McCartney

"My Earth hologram has all positive pixels, allowing my hologram to illuminate my healed desires."

–Linda McCartney

"Here lies my lies. Although I held onto them, I now hold them in the light of truth, and every lie has died."

–Steve Jobs

"I am allowing darkness in my dream, only because I can illuminate it in my mind. I allow it. I illuminate it in my mind with healing thoughts for all involved, and I love myself for healing it in my mind – because it only needs to heal in my mind. I am one with God Mind – all non-love is inconceivable in my universe."

–Steve Jobs

Biographies

Clara Bow was a silent-film superstar nicknamed the "It Girl," whose naturalistic acting style made her one of Hollywood's biggest box-office draws of the 1920s before sound films and studio pressures hastened her withdrawal from acting.

Diana, Princess of Wales was a member of the British royal family whose global influence stemmed from her humanitarian work, particularly with AIDS patients and landmine victims, as well as her highly publicized marriage to Prince Charles.

Laurel and Hardy were a British-American comedy duo whose slow-burn slapstick and contrasting personas made them one of the most enduring teams in film history from the silent era through the 1940s.

Robert F. Kennedy was a U.S. senator, attorney general, and civil rights advocate who played a central role in the John F. Kennedy administration before his assassination during his own 1968 presidential campaign.

Frida Kahlo was a Mexican painter known for deeply personal self-portraits that explored identity, disability, and national culture, often drawing directly from her lifelong physical pain and political beliefs.

Harry Houdini was a Hungarian-born illusionist and escape artist whose death-defying performances and public debunking of fraudulent spiritualists made him one of the most famous entertainers of the early 20th century.

Roberta Flack was an American singer and pianist whose intimate vocal style produced chart-topping hits like 'The First Time Ever I Saw Your Face' and 'Killing Me Softly', earning multiple Grammy Awards.

Jim Croce was a singer-songwriter celebrated for his narrative folk rock songs, whose career was cut short by a fatal plane crash in 1973 at the height of his popularity.

Peter Falk was an American actor best known for portraying the rumpled but incisive detective Columbo, a role that earned him multiple Emmy Awards.

Dean Martin was a singer, actor, and comedian who rose to fame as half of the comedy duo Martin and Lewis before becoming a core member of the Rat Pack and a major solo entertainer.

John Wayne was an American film star whose screen persona became synonymous with Westerns and war films, earning him an Academy Award for *True Grit* late in his career.

Dr. Jane Goodall is a British primatologist whose groundbreaking long-term study of chimpanzees transformed scientific understanding of animal behavior and conservation.

Judy Garland began performing at age 2 and, despite immense professional success, faced lifelong struggles with studio – mandated diet pills, sleep aids, and self – esteem.

Terry, the female Cairn Terrier who played Toto, was a trained animal actor owned by Carl Spitz, and was paid $125 per week, more than the Munchkin actors.

Margaret Hamilton, a former kindergarten teacher, became typecast as a villain but was a dedicated advocate for children and education who often softened her witch persona for young fans.

Ray Bolger was a classically trained dancer who achieved his greatest fame in vaudeville and on Broadway, where his role in *Where's Charley?* earned him a Tony Award.

Jack Haley, a vaudeville and Broadway performer, nearly lost his eyesight from the aluminum powder makeup used for the Tin Man, an allergy that forced a change to an aluminum paste.

Bert Lahr was a major star of burlesque and Broadway, celebrated for his comic persona, and his performance in the play *Waiting for Godot* late in his career earned critical acclaim.

Frank Morgan, born Francis Wuppermann, came from a wealthy family (his father owned the company that made Angostura bitters) and enjoyed a prolific four – decade film career.

Victor Fleming was a former race car driver and cinematographer who was MGM's most trusted director for difficult productions, helming both *The Wizard of Oz* and *Gone with the Wind* in 1939.

King Vidor, a respected and innovative director nominated for five Academy Awards, was brought in to direct the Kansas sequences during a production hiatus.

Billie Burke, a famous Broadway actress, married impresario Florenz Ziegfeld Jr. and successfully transitioned to film, often playing flighty, charming matrons to support their lifestyle after his financial losses.

Charley Grapewin was a veteran character actor whose career spanned from silent films to the 1940s, famously playing Grandpa Joad in *The Grapes of Wrath,* after his role as Uncle Henry.

Clara Blandick was a stage and film actress for over four decades who took her own life in 1962 at age 81, citing failing health as the reason in her suicide note.

Pat Walshe was a little-person actor and former circus performer who appeared in numerous films, often in animalistic roles, and was known for his skill in pantomime.

L. Frank Baum was a prolific author, playwright, and sometime businessman whose series of 14 Oz books became a classic of American children's literature.

Elizabeth Montgomery was an American actress best remembered for her role as Samantha Stephens on the television series *Bewitched*, which ran for eight seasons.

Hedy Lamarr was an Austrian-born actress and inventor who co-developed a frequency-hopping technology during World War II that later became foundational to modern wireless communications.

Rodney Dangerfield was a stand-up comedian and actor whose self-deprecating humor and catchphrase "I don't get no respect" defined his long career.

Bob Marley was a Jamaican singer, songwriter, and global ambassador of reggae music whose work blended spirituality, politics, and social justice.

Humphrey Bogart was an American film actor known for his portrayals of morally complex characters in classics such as *Casablanca* and *The Maltese Falcon*.

Lauren Bacall was an American actress whose husky voice and confident screen presence made her a Hollywood icon, particularly in films opposite Humphrey Bogart, whom she later married.

Clark Gable was one of Hollywood's most prominent leading men, often called "The King of Hollywood," and is best remembered for his role in *Gone with the Wind*.

Carole Lombard was a film actress celebrated for her sharp comedic timing in screwball comedies, whose life ended tragically in a plane crash during World War II.

Albert Einstein was a theoretical physicist whose theory of relativity reshaped modern science and earned him the 1921 Nobel prize in Physics.

Lucille Ball was a pioneering comedian, actress, and television producer whose work on *I Love Lucy* revolutionized sitcom production and reruns.

Sigmund Freud was an Austrian neurologist and the founder of psychoanalysis, whose theories on the unconscious profoundly influenced psychology and Western thought.

William Conrad was an American actor and producer known for his distinctive voice and for starring in television series such as *Cannon*.

Michelangelo was a Renaissance sculptor, painter, and architect whose works – including the Sistine Chapel ceiling and the monumental David and Pieta sculptures – remain among the most influential in Western art.

Frank Lloyd Wright was an American architect who championed organic architecture and designed iconic structures such as Fallingwater and the Guggenheim Museum.

George Orwell was a British writer and journalist whose novels *1984* and *Animal Farm* offered enduring critiques of totalitarianism and political manipulation.

Linda McCartney was a photographer, musician, and animal-rights activist who was a member of the band Wings and the wife of Paul McCartney.

Cleopatra was the last active ruler of Ptolemaic Egypt, known for her political alliances with Julius Caesar and

Mark Antony and her role in Rome's transition from republic to empire.

Elizabeth Taylor was a British-American actress and humanitarian whose film career spanned decades and who later became a leading advocate for HIV/AIDS awareness.

Steve Jobs was a co-founder of Apple Inc. whose emphasis on design and user experience helped shape the modern personal technology industry.

Peter Sellers was a British actor and comedian best known for his versatility and for portraying Inspector Clouseau in *The Pink Panther* film series.

Florence Nightingale was a British nurse and statistician whose work during the Crimean War laid the foundations of modern nursing and hospital sanitation.

About the Author

From God Mind:

*Paul Gorman illuminates as a spiritual researcher,
writing his discoveries into books,
allowing healing in the minds
of all who read them.*

www.ingramcontent.com/pod-product-compliance
Lightning Source LLC
Chambersburg PA
CBHW030906080526
44589CB00010B/177